grow your own

for the

'hungry gap'

Bee and Limnanthes mid-May.

grow your own

for the

'hungry gap'

Trish le Gal

Grow Your Own Books

First published in Great Britain by
Grow Your Own Books
12 Northfield Avenue
Wells-next-the-Sea
Norfolk NR23 1LL
www.growyourownbooks.co.uk

A catalogue record of this book is
available from the British Library

ISBN 978-0-9565724-0-0

Designed by Trish le Gal
Printed by Crowes Printers
www.crowes.co.uk

Contents

Foreword

One cabbage. That is where it started. With just one cabbage. One of those with the dark green outer leaves, so fresh that it squeaks when cut, layers of colours from olive, lime, and daffodil yellow, moisture beading between each layer. Gently simmered, steam rising from the plate. When did cabbage ever taste this good!

This 'one cabbage' was handed to me after a long walk with my lurcher Millie, across the beautiful marshes on the North Norfolk coast. I had stumbled across Trish and her oasis of allotments; rows of perfumed lavender and rosemary, lush crops of parsley, shiny spinach, spurs of swaying artichoke heads and growing willow seats.

My visits became more frequent; my load getting heavier each time. My knowledge of the produce and our friendship sprouted like the seedlings in the pots. Vegetables and herbs began appearing on my doorstep. Just like Christmas, each newspaper-wrapped parcel was undone to reveal a variety of vegetables, some completely unknown to me. Even now, four years later, I still unwrap each one and lay them all out on the kitchen surface admiring the colours, the shapes, the dust, the dirt, the mud and the odd wriggling bug! Chard which is still wet from that morning's shower, the misshapen carrots, so sweet and so tender, and the perfume of freshly picked tomatoes.

I enjoy the challenge of planning my meals around the vegetables offered. I scour my many cookbooks for new recipes. This one-time supermarket shopper now has an awareness of the seasonal vegetable, an appreciation of the value of organic production and locally grown food. However, flavour remains the stronger influence and quite clearly you reap what you sow. I have learnt, without evangelism, the methods and skills used, the time and care taken to cultivate this produce.

Running my own business does not allow me the time for my own allotment but I gratefully share the bounty. I do admire the dedication and sheer hard work and trust me it's worth it, the vegetables are so very, very good.

Start with the cabbage!

Jill Ward

Opposite: Calendula, the ideal companion.

Introduction

This book is for you if you have had some success with growing vegetables to eat in the summer, autumn and early winter and now want to fill the 'hungry gap' months of late winter to late spring.

For the purposes of planning, I have taken these months to be March, April and May. Depending on the severity of the winter and the warmth of the spring, this period can overlap as far back as January and sneak its way into June. This is one third of the year when the majority of the population is, to a large extent, dependent on imported food. This need not be so.

The information here is based on my own experience of trying to make it through the year without resorting to air-mile/ herbicide/ pesticide supported vegetables obtained through the supermarket system. The first few years of trying to support my small family of three found us shopping down the road for other organic locally grown potatoes and onions with far too many broad beans and courgettes in the freezer. Although it is possible to achieve success with straightforward crops like rhubarb, leeks, and kale in the first year of trying, it has taken me about ten years to achieve anything remotely like a balance.

There are many comprehensive gardening books available and I have a fair few of them, but I found that, in order to produce enough vegetables of sufficient variety I needed at least five or six of them out at once. I would make lists, work backwards to seed-sowing dates, get out the seed catalogues, and sift through them for the right varieties. Surely it would be better, I thought, to have the information all in the one place. Hence this guide.

Chapter one contains comments on equipment, heritage vegetables and basic seed-saving, the bed system, crop rotation and fertility, crop protection, and the lunar calendar. I grow organically.

Chapter two includes vegetables I have grown to eat fresh or stored without using additional resources. I describe how we like to eat them, their place in the rotation, preferred soil type and situation. Suggestions are made about particularly successful varieties, sowing, planting, harvesting and caring for the crop throughout the year. There is an 'afterword' for each, and this is intended to help you make ready for the next crop. Absences include swede, salsify and scorzonera. These are on my 'must try harder' list. Sprouting seeds are not covered although we do do this and they are a welcome addition. Others are more knowledgeable about these than I am.

Chapter three includes comments on herbs available in the hungry gap.

Chapter four includes limited suggestions for dealing with summer gluts. These are vegetable 'desirables' that we eat throughout the winter and spring after processing. Favourite recipes are suggested. The idea is that, should our oil-based economy come to a shuddering halt, then this chapter will become redundant. Alternatively, the processes used in it will be supported by sustainable sources of energy.

Anyone gardening north, south or west of Norfolk will need to accommodate seasonal variation in temperature and differences in rainfall when following my planting advice. I took the photographs throughout the year on my allotments in North Norfolk.

Opposite: Salad in March.

Purple Sprouting broccoli seedlings in April.

Chapter 1
get ready to grow

What tools to use

You need at least some tools for any form of gardening. Container gardening probably requires the least, but then you do need pots, or bags, or boxes. Hungry gap gardening involves a list common to all forms of gardening with a few additions.

A spade, fork, hoe, hand trowel and rake are basics. Secateurs are a must for cutting down raspberries and pruning fruit trees and some herbs. A dibber for planting out leeks, and sometimes brassicas, is also to my mind essential. You will need something to cut the grass with if you have grass paths. Trays and pots of various sizes are necessary for setting seeds and growing on seedlings. Labels are more important than you might imagine and can also function as mini trench-makers used on their side in a tray and as mini dibbers when pricking out. You will need some means of support for climbing peas and beans if you choose to grow these, and stakes for tomatoes. A D-cutter for keeping the edges of the paths defined is easier to use for this task than a spade. A sieve for getting the lumps out of homemade compost comes in handy though probably doesn't count as essential. A line can be useful, although in practice I hardly ever use one. I also find a bulb planter very efficient and easy on my back to use when planting potatoes and transplants in 9cm pots, but you could manage with a trowel, or a spade, or a hoe.

My planting stick is very important to me. As I use the 'bed system', the stick is as long as the width of a bed which is just over a metre. It is triangular in cross-section with one side of the triangle much shorter than the other two sides which taper to a sharp edge. I can't remember how I came by it. It is wooden and the kind of battening that builders throw away once their work is finished. The sharp edge is pressed down into the prepared soil to make drills for seeds that are sown directly into the soil such as carrot, parsnip, beetroot and leek seeds. Using the stick repeatedly, I make grids across and down the beds to position onion sets, garlic, lettuce seedlings and dwarf bean seedlings. If you use a draw hoe and line that works fine too.

Equipment to do with water is becoming increasingly important as rainfall becomes unpredictable. Barrels to hold water and liquid feed and watering cans (two to make life easier for your shoulders) are the minimum. Compost bins are essential; three if you can manage it, one being added to, one being emptied and one 'cooking'. I am privileged to have a wormery with a tap at the bottom to draw off the liquid that, diluted, keeps my pea shoots going all winter.

Some form of cover for starting early in the season and going on late will help you grow for the hungry gap. This can be as simple as a sunny window sill. Cloches made from wire and plastic are a step up. Also useful are covers of shading and other netted fabrics to give protection from wind, insects, and birds. Cold frames are easy to make from recycled timber and windows once you have a pattern and this is easily found in any number of gardening books. A greenhouse is great for both summer and winter growing. One suggestion is to 'put the word out' and wait until someone is down-sizing or up-grading and they no longer have a use for theirs. We got ours for a very reasonable price from a neighbour and walked the aluminium

Opposite: My hoe.

frame over to the plot. Luckily, our allotments tend not to have a problem with vandalism, but fences to filter the wind did have to be constructed first, as the frame on a small greenhouse will twist and the glass will shatter. A polytunnel is also desirable. Although it may seem like a luxury, it is one that will pay for itself in less than five years. If you like to raise all your own plants from seed a heated propagator is necessary, especially for celeriac and tomatoes.

Buckets or tubs for forcing rhubarb and seakale are a must for April and May harvests. Mine are over a metre tall for the rhubarb and around 40cm for the seakale but capacity will depend on the vigour of your plants. Your local council may sell black plastic compost bins that work well for rhubarb.

You will need storage space for onions, garlic, squash and any roots that you lift.

From the top: My planting stick, greenhouse at sunrise, rhubarb forcing tub, homemade cloche in April.

What seeds to sow

Some of the vegetables I grow are old favourites (for example Musselburgh leeks) and have been maintained on seed lists for years. However, at least fifty percent of the vegetables I grow are known loosely as heritage varieties, those that have fallen off the bottom of mainstream seed company lists. As I like to save my own seed I seldom grow hybrid varieties, although I can be tempted by F1 brassicas, and will take advantage of plant-breeding research for blight resistance (Sarpo potatoes) and flavour (Sungold F1 tomatoes).

One of the advantages of saving your own seed is that the vegetables become acclimatised, which can lead to improved germination and increased yield. If, however, you have a small garden and are a bit pushed for space, then keeping the vegetables in the ground until flowering and seed setting can be a disadvantage. In this case you may be restricted to saving seed from varieties either as you harvest them to eat or just a little bit later (tomatoes, peas, beans). Another advantage is that the vegetables often have more and different flavours from those we have become accustomed to. I haven't been able to convert my partner to the taste of open-pollinated sweet corn for example, but for me, every time we have it, I re-live the taste of the hot New Zealand summers of my childhood. Yet another advantage of heritage varieties is that they come to maturity over an extended period and lessen the likelihood of 'gluts'.

Membership of the Heritage Seed Library (HSL) and Garden Organic has enabled me to source, and exchange with other gardeners, carrot, bean, pea, tomato, cabbage, kale and other seed over a period of years such that my own stock has increased. It is a wonderful service and very empowering.

There are a number of publications and seed suppliers that support this move to self-sufficiency, for example, 'Back Garden Seed Saving', and 'Heritage Vegetables' by Sue Stickland. Some seed companies actually send out seed saving instructions with the varieties that you order. See the Resources section of this book for further information.

Above: Gladstone peas.
Below: Red Brunswick onion seeds.

The bed system

My beds measure just over a metre wide and between 5 to 10 metres long. They are oriented north to south with the plants set in short rows or grids across the beds. I find this makes for easy hoeing and weeding. Keeping a bed trim and under control is less daunting than facing the whole plot all at once. Not treading on the beds, with continuous additions of compost and manure, results in the beds forming a natural mound.

There is a trend towards raising beds with recycled plastic or wooden boards but this is not necessary on my type of soil which is a sandy loam over chalk. I have tried it but found slugs and snails like to over-winter in the crevices and couch grass likes to hug and travel along the edges making it difficult to weed out. Raised beds are also expensive to set up. However, if you have clay soil or garden using a wheelchair then beds raised with boards might be the answer.

My paths are less than half a metre wide. I find that keeping the paths mulched (with straw, cardboard, shredded paper and sometimes all three) and weed-free is very important psychologically.

If you use a rotavator or, as some on my site do, have the whole plot cultivated with a tractor each year in early spring, then only some of what I offer in this book will apply. In the spring we are eating hungry gap produce, and many of the beds are still full.

Top: A view of some beds in the last week in May.
Middle: Maincrop potatoes and beetroot in the first week in June.
Bottom: Maincrop onions nearly ready for lifting at the end of July.

Crop rotation & fertility

There are two main reasons for crop rotation. The first and primary reason is to resist the persistence of family specific diseases. For example, white rot in onions and blight in potatoes and tomatoes. In the polytunnel and greenhouse, where much of the space is dedicated to members of the Solanaceae (tomatoes, peppers, aubergines), disease in the soil can be a particular problem. Some gardeners take these crops out of the soil and into pots to give the borders a rest.

The second reason for rotation is that related crops use specific nutrients and minerals and these can become depleted.

My rotation plan is as follows: potatoes, legumes, brassicas, onions, roots. I usually fill in with lettuces or green manure (phaecelia or Hungarian rye) and grow another rotation 'neutral' crop at the end of this sequence like sweetcorn or cucumbers or squash. Then I start again: PLBOR. I find note-taking falls to the bottom of my list of things to do, so try to stick firmly to this order so that I know what to set out next. If you can't manage this long a sequence, just remember to plant something different in the same bit of ground each year.

Potato: Peppers, potatoes, tomatoes, tomatillos.

Legume: Beans and peas.

Brassica: Broccoli, brussels sprouts, cabbage, cauliflower, Chinese leaves, cress, kale, radish, seakale, swede, turnip.

Onion: Garlic, leeks, onions.

Roots: Beetroot, carrots, celeriac, parsnips.

Neutral: Chard, chicory, endive, lettuce, squash.

Vegetables included in the neutral rotation do belong to families of course, but their diseases are not sufficiently problematic for most of us to worry about. Rotation also becomes a concern for 'permanents' such as artichokes (Compositae) and asparagus (Liliaceae/onion rotation) when clearing or moving them.

Note that some herbs are included in the rotation (parsley in the roots, chives in the onions), some are permanent and replaced every few years (sage, rosemary, thyme), and some are 'neutral'.

Rotation and rejuvenation of the soil with compost, animal and green manures with adjustments for acidity and alkalinity ensures a continuing healthy balance. I grow phaecelia as a green manure because it is easy and neutral in the rotation. Nutrients are retained that would otherwise leach readily from my sandy soil. Dig it in when it is 15-20cm high about a month before sowing seeds. Leave it to flower in the spring and it will attract pollinators to the plot when there are few other flowers about. This helps with broad bean pollination in particular.

The benefits of comfrey are widely recognised. I use it as a mulch and rotted down under a little water to provide a liquid manure. If you grow Bocking 14 then the plants do not spread by seeding. Take care when hoeing around the plants though as new plants will grow from any roots you cut through. This also means you can extend your bed by taking sections of root 2-3cm long and planting them elsewhere.

Top: Phaecelia planted as a green manure.

Middle: Building a compost heap from fresh horse manure, comfrey and water. Cover lastly with black plastic.

Bottom: Comfrey leaf at the 'heart' of plot fertility.

Opposite: Small fires along the beds add ash for root crops.

Crop protection

The width of my beds suits the way I protect my crops from wind, birds, flying insects, slugs and snails. Pigeons and rabbits are a particular problem in early spring. I have many methods and you will find a variety of structures available to buy. Netting and wire recycled or bought new are useful.

My current favoured method of protecting spring cabbages against pigeons is single bed frames stripped to the frame and painted with preservative. They are covered with brassica netting anchored with staples or small nails. Rope handles tacked to each end help with lifting them away for hoeing and harvesting. Covered with fleece and placed over carrots, these frames also provide protection against carrot fly.

Another suggestion for winter brassicas (cauli, cabbage, sprouting broccoli and kale) is lengths of plumbing pipe stretched across the bed about a metre apart (see p. 53). The length of the pipe is adjusted to the height the crop is expected to grow and the width of the fabric you are using. The pipes are held in place by 40cm lengths of bamboo, half of each is pushed into the pipe with the other half pushed into the ground. A length of fabric is stretched over the hoops down the bed and anchored at the ends and sides with lengths of wood or metal. Slugs tend to 'hide' under the wood so it is easy to collect and deal with them from here. Stretching lengths of string over the fabric near to each hoop helps the structure to stay secure. Paying attention to the lowest anchor points will allow you to lift each edge for access to weed, hoe or harvest. This system stands up to the wind fairly well in our area although I have gone down after a gale to find the green fabric protection for my winter leaves wrapped around the bean poles in the next bed.

Pests vary and I'm sure you will have your own problems to solve. One spring I watched a mother rabbit access her nursery burrow under some large chard plants, re-emerge and pat the soil back into place. Not wanting a family of little ones running around, I dug out the set and disposed of them. The next year I was ready for this, observed a burrow in construction, waited a couple of weeks, and did the same. I have also witnessed a rabbit on its hind legs gnawing through a wire barrier. Thankfully I don't have a problem with larger animals such as deer or badgers, although human pests have been known to bother my raspberries.

The most serious disease I encounter is blight. Tomatoes are impossible outside and I grow Sarpo potatoes as a main crop. When blight hits the early potatoes I cut the tops off and bag them up for the council recycling centre. I harvest the tubers that the plants have managed to produce a couple of weeks later. The harvest of first early potatoes signals to me that the hungry gap is truly over.

Some years mildew on the onions will come after light rain following a long dry spell. At this point I water the plants until they are thoroughly damp and this appears to help them cope.

Some weeds in particular harbour pests and diseases. Groundsel is notorious for over-wintering aphids: it also gets rust. There are several very good publications around on weeds, pests and diseases (Resources; p.144-145).

Opposite: Cabbage white caterpillar.

Workflow

Some gardeners seem to know when to put in their winter cabbages or maincrop potatoes, so one sort of advice would be to watch others who get results, and do what they do. It is also easy to be overwhelmed, especially in spring when everything seems to need doing at once.

Given that only a few gardeners grow more than a basic range of vegetables on my site, and that doing more than one thing at a time is not possible, I use the biodynamic (lunar) calendar (Resources; p.146) to advise me. I also suspect that the earth is not part of the universe for nothing, and that the influence of the moon and other planets on soil water and bio-rhythms is maybe something we once knew and have drifted away from.

Briefly, the annual calendar is divided into the periods between each full moon. Each of these is further divided into two; a planting period and a non-planting period, each of about 14 days. This is tied to the waxing and waning of the moon and the relative positions of the planets and whether you live in the Northern or Southern hemisphere.

Within these 14 day periods there are days auspicious for tending to plants that are categorised depending on the part of the plant that we eat; roots, flowers, leaves and fruits. Sometimes these periods last for 2-3 days and sometimes a few hours only. During the root planting period I set carrots, parsnips, potatoes and leeks for example, and ignore all the

other tasks that need doing. During the flower period sprouting broccoli and companion plants are sown. During the leaf period lettuce and other leaves go in, and during the fruit period seeds of peas, beans and tomatoes.

It's not completely straightforward. For example, Maria Thun's research suggests that, whereas sprouting broccoli does best planted on flower days, cauliflower does best on leaf days.

During the non-planting periods I attend to the appropriate crop hoeing and mulching as required. There are also 'do-nothing' days when I get to build cold frames, or simply have a rest. One friend of mine said that these are the only days of the calendar she truly follows! Another suggested that if events get in the way she just sets her seeds whenever she can get into the garden and her garden does thrive.

There are also biodynamic preparations that you can spray at certain times to promote healthy growth and yield. Preparations are still a mystery to me. Every now and then I attempt to 'go there' but haven't quite made it yet. However, I have used the planting calendar to good effect for 10 years, and can recommend it simply on the basis of stress relief and the healthy-looking plants you see in this book.

Below: Moonrise over the marshes, a short walk from the allotments.

Lettuce seedlings in October to plant out under cover.

Chapter 2
A-Z fresh or stored

Artichoke-globe

Cynara scolymus

Even though these take up a lot of space I grow several plants to ensure enough for three people at once. Our preference is to eat these steamed. I have tried small ones chargrilled and preserved in lemon juice and oil which was moderately successful. For a very special occasion I can be persuaded to peel them back to the hearts and poach them in white wine and olive oil with peas, beans and herbs to make a salad that is delicious eaten warm.

Rotation
Permanent. Move every four to five years.

Soil
Well drained and rich.

Situation
Sunny and sheltered, although a certain amount of breeze will help deter infestations of blackfly.

Varieties
I started my patch from seeds of Green Globe and Romanesco. There are other varieties that are said to be superior such as Vert de Laon.

Sow
Sow one seed per 9cm pot in April.

Plant
Settle the small seedlings into a pot the next size up and over-winter in a cold frame. Set the plants out as for offsets. It is best to take offsets from plants that you know give fine buds. Most people do this in the spring selecting shoots and separating them from the parent plant with a sharp knife or spade, making sure there is a piece of root attached. Prepare your planting holes about 80cm apart each with a shovel full of manure and a good tablespoon of bone meal if you have it. Mix well with the spade. Set each plant so that the shoot will be about 8cm below the surface of the soil when you are finished. Fill the hole with a watering can full of water and allow it to drain away. Fill in the soil around the plant and firm it in with your hands. The offsets can be quite robust and I have been successful in September with this method. They looked dreadful for the first week or so but picked up after this.

Care
Keep them weed-free. They grow into such enormous plants that they suppress most weeds after the first few weeks. I mound straw and manure around them over the winter and this both feeds them and protects them from low temperatures.

Harvest
The first few buds arrive early in May. Harvest them at the stage you like to eat them. Some people prefer the baby ones and others like to leave them until they are a bit more mature. We like any stage. A 5cm stalk is usual. If you have to keep them, cut a longer stalk and put them in a tub of water.

Afterword
Digging these out at the end of five years can be a tough job. Make sure you get as much of the root as you can and leave the bed to rest for a few months so that you can remove any pieces that re-shoot. From this point I either prepare for a neutral crop (add more muck and plant sweetcorn) or move back into the rotation (add nothing and set beetroot).

Opposite: Flower bud in mid-May.

Artichoke-Jerusalem

Heliathus tuberosus

I love this vegetable. To me the taste is sweet and nutty and the after-effects (wind) are mild. For others however, who also love the taste, the after-effects are cruel. I have heard that eating a small amount early in the season prepares the gut to digest them, and that building up your gut flora gradually eases the problem. Cooking with turmeric is also supposed to help. If there is no problem, artichoke soup is wonderful as are roast artichokes, or artichokes par-boiled and sweated with butter and garlic. Some people eat them raw sliced into salads.

Rotation

Permanent. All tubers are lifted annually and selected ones are replanted. Weed out all 'volunteers' to continue to produce large tubers.

Soil

Almost any soil will do but well-drained and rich is best for big tubers.

Situation

They will tolerate a bit of shade but in full sun they will do better. It is possible to use them to protect other crops from the wind but they are heavy feeders and will take from their neighbours.

Varieties

After growing both the knobbly garden variety and Fuseau which is smoother skinned and easier to peel, I would suggest that growing the knobbly ones is a waste of time. If you don't know anyone who will give you half a dozen Fuseau tubers to start your own patch, spend out and order some.

Sow

Not from seed.

Plant

Any time from February to April. Choose the smoothest and largest tubers to re-plant. Set them with the sprouting end up and cover with about 15cm of soil. If you space them 30cm apart you will get medium-sized tubers; 60cm apart will give you large ones.

Care

Weed them early on. Later they out-compete most weeds. Jerusalem artichokes rarely get pests and diseases. The young shoots and occasionally the tubers may need some protection from rabbits. The plants can grow up to two metres tall and when the autumn winds come I cut the foliage down to about 60cm to prevent wind-rock.

Harvest

Dig tubers as you need them from February or even before this. Be careful to get every last one as those you leave will re-grow. Do not compost the waste as the stalks take a long time to break down. I submerge un-wanted tubers in a tub of water to rot and burn the stalks after tying a few short lengths into bundles to provide over-wintering homes for lacewings. A chipper-shredder would be good for the stalks but not the tubers. If you want to clear the bed store the tubers in sand or used compost to prevent dehydration and keep the boxes somewhere cool and dark.

Afterword

After clearing the bed dig large holes where you will be re-planting. Put a shovel full of manure in each and mix it up with the soil before setting your new tubers.

Opposite: Fuseau tubers photographed in March.

Asparagus

Asparagus officinalis

This is the supreme treat vegetable of the hungry gap. I have met only one person who doesn't like it, so it is possible, though difficult for me to understand. My mature plants push up their first tender shoots in the middle of April and I cut until the end of the first week in June. Prepare them by washing. Trim off the tough outer stem of the base (usually about the bottom 5cm) with a potato peeler or sharp knife. This avoids stringy bits while you are eating. We eat it steamed and served hot with butter or cold with vinaigrette and sometimes baked with a drizzle of olive oil. If you have very few spears, adding them late to pasta or risotto together with shreds of parma ham is tasty, and if you have a 'glut' there are always soups and soufflés to be made. It also freezes beautifully. Steam for two to three minutes, cool rapidly in iced water, dry them off on a clean tea towel and free-flow freeze the spears on trays before packing them into a freezer bag. From frozen, asparagus spears are best done in the oven.

Rotation
Permanent (onion family). They crop well for more than 15 years.

Soil
Well drained, sandy and moderately rich. To build a raised bed use loam, leaf mould, sand and a little lime (don't use lime on chalky soils).

Situation
Full sun. Avoid areas that frost badly and provide some protection from the wind to prevent wind-rock.

Varieties
If you grow from seed you will be restricted to Connover's Colossal but I am so far very pleased with mine that are now coming into their fourth year. There is a big saving on cost if you grow from seed. Alternatively you can buy one, two, or three year old crowns of either Connover's Colossal or a variety of male hybrids. I grow Fileas, Franklim and Grolim cultivars.

Sow
Seed in April in a tray of multipurpose compost and prick out into 9cm pots. Grow them on for a year, over-wintering them in an open cold frame. Each plant will produce 2 to 5 shoots from a crown that has spaghetti-like roots.

Plant
Most books recommend that you don't grow asparagus from seed because you don't know whether you'll get male or female plants. You want males. I've found it difficult to buy a batch of purely male plants though – there always seem to be one or two that have berries and the incidence of female plants in the ones I seeded is low. However, different cultivars will spread the season a week or two either way. When your crowns arrive soak them for an hour before setting them into a well-mucked 23cm deep trench on a small mound in the bottom of the trench. Arrange each plant so that its roots spread out spider-like down the sides of the mound. Plant them 30cm apart with 60cm between rows. Water them in and cover so that they are level with the soil. Mulch the new bed to deter weeds.

Care
It is very important to keep the bed weed-free as asparagus does not like competition. Support the tall fronds with a rope so that they don't get blown over and cut them down to just

Opposite: Asparagus in April.

above the ground when the fronds turn yellow. I mulch with well-rotted manure one year and seaweed the next. In the second year I feed with comfrey in late February, early March to give them a boost. In a dry spring I give the beds a good soaking with water once or twice if I have the time. Asparagus beetle is the worst pest I encounter. Watch out for them in May and squash them, check also for 2mm torpedo-shaped eggs attached to the stems and rub these off. Alternatively, catch them at the larval stage later or they will strip the leaves and weaken the plants. A friend found that the beetles accumulated in beer traps he set out for slugs.

Harvest

Cut them the length you like – this is usually 12-16cm long – at the base of the spear 3-4cm below ground level with a sharp knife. A grapefruit knife works well and is much cheaper than the specialist knife you can buy. Take care not to sever new shoots coming through. Don't crop plants younger than three years old and stop in late May for four to five year old plants. I've seen an over-cropped asparagus bed and it is not a pretty sight.

Afterword

Choose fresh ground when starting a new asparagus bed to protect against disease. Return the spent asparagus bed to the rotation.

Below: A well established asparagus bed in November with foliage just starting to yellow.

Beans

Phaseolus vulgaris

Dried beans are a staple in the hungry gap and we enjoy them in a variety of dishes. The beans are soaked to fatten them up again, either overnight, or for a couple of hours before they are required if they are quite fresh. Cover them with water and bring to the boil. Drain and add fresh water and a tablespoon of winter savoury if you have it. The winter savoury, fresh or dried, adds flavour and makes the beans more digestible. Boil them until they are soft or add them partially cooked to soups, casseroles, boiling ham and so on. Fully cooked they can be made into salads with other beans and finely chopped vegetables. Paté is good. Blend the beans with garlic, olive oil, lemon juice, salt and pepper and serve on toast or stuffed into pitta bread with salad or coleslaw. One of our dried bean favourites is Mexican re-fried beans with all the trimmings. We have particular friends who like to be alerted when we make this kind of meal.

Rotation
Legume.

Soil
Medium rich and well-drained.

Situation
Sunny. They will tolerate some shade and it depends upon when in the season you start them off. Early and late, they will need full sun. In the polytunnel you may find that they suffer from the heat if you haven't been early enough starting them off.

Varieties
There are three main types for hungry gap growing. The low-growing (30-50cm tall) varieties I have tried are Horsehead, Orca (Yin Yang) and Negritos. A climbing French bean (2m) called Old Homestead is particularly good as a dual purpose (picked small for fresh use throughout the summer and left to use dried for later). Cherokee Trail of Tears has beautiful and tasty medium-sized black beans and is also a climbing French type. Bosnian is a climbing flat type and best used as a drying bean although the young pods can be eaten fresh. This last is very similar to Borlotti but I find the yield is greater in my situation.

Sow
Individual seeds in root trainers or 9cm pots under cover in May. It is a waste of time my setting seeds outdoors where I live, as bean seed fly spoils them as they germinate. You may not have this pest however, and sowing outdoors, after all danger of frost has passed will yield a good crop. For dwarf types sow seeds 10-15cm apart, 5cm deep in rows 30-40cm apart, for climbing types sow15cm apart against supporting canes and netting.

Plant
Do this when you are sure the weather will be warm enough in your area. Beans are very sensitive to low temperatures. In North Norfolk this is around the first week in June. For climbing types, put your climbing support in place and dig deep holes (use a bulb planter if you have one) so that there is plenty of room for the roots and water them in well. Firm the soil around the roots once the water has drained away. Fifteen to 20cm between plants for the climbers and 20cm for dwarf types will maximise the yield per plant. I use canes or

other poles for support and, as I never seem to have enough, drape the poles with 10cm squared plastic netting. Additional support at both ends of my double wigwam rows is necessary as the structure is vulnerable to the wind once covered in foliage.

Care

Keep them reasonably well-weeded. Mulching the paths and in between the plants with grass clippings helps to conserve moisture. If the weather is very dry all beans will benefit from additional water.

Harvest

Old Homestead can be picked throughout the summer as it is prolific given the right weather conditions and will still yield enough for drying. However, apart from a first pick to encourage fruiting, all the others can be left alone until maturity. When the plants start to lose their leaves pull up the dwarf French whole. Tie them in bunches and hang under cover to complete drying. For the climbers, strip the beans from the vines and lay them flat in a single layer on a breathable surface outside if you are certain it won't rain (a light shower won't hurt). Alternatively, bring them in somewhere warm. An old sheet on the tiled floor of our conservatory gets moved out on a fine day and brought in at night. Pod them when the shells are crisp and lay the seeds out for a while to finish off. If you leave picking them too late some of the pods may split open, and if you don't give them enough air while drying they can go mouldy.

Afterword

Clear the canes and debris from the beds and either sow with a green manure to turn under in spring, or cover the bed with well rotted manure or compost to feed the brassicas that will follow.

Opposite: Climbing French bean Cherokee Trail of Tears at the end of August.
Over left: Yin Yang after harvest at the end of August.
Over right: Climbing beans intercropped with lettuces on the 25th May.

Beetroot

Beta vulgaris

We like to eat this, but I'm not very good at growing it for the hungry gap. I think that the mistake I make is that I underestimate how much nourishment the roots actually require. Most of the books say not much. I also tend to sow too early for roots that will grow big enough to last in the ground or lift for storage. When we have it, the older adult in my family likes it the traditional way boiled, sliced and with a little vinegar and sugar. Roasted they are delicious. Grated raw with horseradish and yoghurt is a favourite. Soup is good.

Rotation
Roots.
Soil
Not too rich.
Situation
Well-drained and sunny.
Varieties
Barabietola di Chiggia, Bolthardy, Carillon (hard to find but this one was very successful for me), Cylindra, and Sanguina. In addition to these, I tried white beetroot one year and while reasonably successfully grown, we were slow to eat it. A blind taste-test revealed that the flavour was fine! I haven't yet tried single-seeded (monogerm) varieties.
Sow
April to July directly into the soil. Set seed around 8cm apart in drills 2.5cm deep with rows about 30cm apart. You could try setting seed into modules and transplanting them but I have had limited success with this.
Plant
Set module sown plants 10-15cm apart.
Care
Leaf spotting can be controlled by adding wood ash to the bed before planting. Keep young plants well weeded and moist. Thin the young seedlings to one every 10-15cm. Cover with straw from late autumn or lift and store not touching in moist peat or sand.
Harvest
From store, or lift when needed as the weather allows.
Afterword
Set green manure or cover the beds with well-rotted manure ready for potatoes to follow.

Left: Sanguina seedlings mid-May.
Opposite: Sanguina roots mid-June.

Broccoli

Brassica oleracea Italica Group

Purple sprouting broccoli is our absolute favourite spring vegetable. We have the shoots steamed, or with a light cheese sauce, or if people are coming to eat and there aren't many shoots to go around, added late to pasta.

Rotation
Brassica.

Soil
Rich and well-drained. Muck well over the winter after removing pea and bean hulms. Add lime if you need to, but not at the same time as the manure.

Situation
Sunny.

Varieties
I grow both early and late varieties. Shoots from the early variety come in March and from the late, 3-4 weeks later. As the plants take up a lot of space I commit to the purple as it is supposed to be higher yielding but there is a white variety which some people prefer. I have seen substantial crops on the white variety on a neighbour's plot. I'm trying Claret F1 this year to see if I can extend the season even later.

Sow
April or May in a 9cm pot in multi-purpose compost. Alternatively sow a short row across a seed tray with other brassicas that have a similar germination time to save space. Seeds can also be sown outside in a seed-bed or an open coldframe but I have best success from a pot.

Plant
Prick out pot or seedtray sown seedlings when they are large enough to handle, into compost around 10cm deep. Place the young seedlings 10cm apart and grow them on until they are about 8-10cm tall and substantial enough to deter minor slug and snail attack. Thin young seedbed seedlings to12cm or so apart and grow these on till they are 8-10cm tall. The final planting needs to be in firm ground so if you must fork over the bed before transplanting, tread it back down. Set the young plants out so that the seed leaves are at the level of the soil in holes about 60cm apart. Water them in, let the water drain and firm the soil around them well.

Care
A number of pests love brassica plants. Cover the young plants with mesh fine enough to stop butterflies later in the season. Leave enough room so that their growth is not restricted and leave yourself access to hoe and weed. Cabbage root fly may sometimes give trouble: look out for yellowing plants and investigate the roots. There are a number of devices on the market to protect against these; split circles of underlay pushed around the stems work reasonably well. Be aware that pigeons and rabbits will also have a go. The plants can grow very tall (this year mine are easily 1.3m – over 4ft) and run the risk of lodging (falling over). This tends to lower the yield so support them with stakes if they need it. Some people find earthing-up the stems helps. Whitefly can be a bit of a problem but I hose it off rather than resort to sprays. If you keep the bed hoed well at the beginning of their growth,

Opposite: First Early Sprouting Broccoli in late February.

broccoli make such big plants that subsequent weeds are suppressed.

Harvest

Simply snap off the shoots as they come. The sideshoots will grow away and get smaller and smaller but they will still be delicious.

Afterword

When the plants have finished producing, dig them up roots and all, and bash or slice the stems with a spade before composting. Prepare the beds for leeks or onions by adding compost or a light amount of manure.

Brussels sprouts

Brassica oleracae Gemmifera Group

I have become a fan of these since discovering that own-grown sprouts taste nothing like the bought ones. We eat them shredded finely in coleslaw or stir-fried, combined with chestnuts, or steamed the traditional way to accompany roast dinners.

Rotation
Brassica.

Soil
Medium rich and firm.

Site
Sunny.

Varieties
Choose a late variety such as Seven Hills that will stand until the middle of March.

Sow
In April set a few seeds in a 9cm pot and germinate under cover or outside in an open cold frame.

Plant
When the small seedlings are large enough to handle, prick them out into modules or into a tray of multi-purpose compost 7-8cm deep. A tip for when you are handling all young seedlings is to pick them up by their leaves only. Do not touch the stems. If a leaf breaks off the plant will grow another. If the stem is damaged the whole plant is destroyed. Grow the young sprouts on until they are at least 10-12cm tall. Prepare ground manured over winter by forking it over and then tramp the soil down hard before setting out your young plants. Make holes with a dibber, trowel or bulb planter 80-90cm apart, and set out your plants so that the seed leaves are level with the soil. Water them in thoroughly and let the water drain away. Press the soil back around the roots very firmly.

Care
Keep them well-hoed and protected from all the usual brassica pests. Pigeons are a particular nuisance in the spring. If you plant coriander nearby and allow it to flower it will attract hoverflies that feast on aphids. Staking even short varieties or mounding the soil up around the stems will help to stop them lodging (falling over).

Harvest
Pick buds from the bottom up.

Afterword
Fork out the roots and bash the stems before adding them to the compost heap. Clear the beds and prepare for maincrop onions by adding a small amount of manure or compost.

Opposite: Brussels sprouts in March showing pigeon damage.

Cabbage

Brassica oleracea Capitata Group

According to the seed catalogues it is perfectly possible to have cabbage all the year round. Here are some that should serve you for March, April and May with a bit of practice. My fondness for cabbage has increased in direct proportion to my realisation that growing a good cabbage when you want it requires more than a modicum of skill. Here I have learned from the 'old ones' on the plot. These are men usually, who have been growing brassicas since digging for victory and who excel at it. We eat cabbage in coleslaw, steamed, stir-fried, curried with tomatoes that have been free-flow frozen (courtesy of a recipe from Madhur Jaffrey), and in bubble-and-squeak. One member of my family is very fond of pickled red cabbage. This small list scrapes the surface of what people do and have done with cabbage.

Rotation
Brassica.

Soil
Richer than you would imagine, free-draining, firm and well-limed.

Situation
Full sun to do well.

Varieties
There are two main types of cabbage of interest here. First are the 'spring' cabbages that are sown in late summer (August/September) for harvest in spring. Two examples you see pictured here are Peter F1 and a loose-leaved variety called Delaway that was obtained from the person in Ireland who maintains it for the Heritage Seed Library. There are many varieties of spring cabbage and they are identified clearly in the seed catalogues as such. Second are the 'winter' cabbages sown in late spring (April/May) and which occupy their stations in the beds for most of the year, growing slowly towards a harvest in late winter. Examples are Tundra F1 (sometimes stands until late April), Vertus (a savoy type that is harvested from December till February and, if you are lucky, it will stand), Holland Late Winter (a white cabbage ready in December and suitable for storing) and January King (a savoy type that may be ready from December and later). I have found some variation from catalogue suggestions about harvesting times. When you set the seed, how wet and warm the season is, and whether or not you fancy cabbage sufficiently to cut it before it is ready all come into play.

Sow
Your timing will vary according to variety (see above). Try the seedbed method if you are good at this. Draw out 2cm deep drills in an area that is easy to keep an eye on and sow seed thinly. However, if you are still feeling your way, sprinkle a few seeds of your chosen variety in a 9cm pot and germinate them outdoors. I have an open cloche with some brassica netting thrown over it near my shed for seeds like this. Don't let them dry out. Choose 2-3 types to start off with; one spring, one winter and one red maybe, depending on what you like to eat.

Plant
Prick out your tiny seedlings into 6-8cm deep multipurpose compost or modules to grow them on until they have 4-5 leaves beyond their seed

Opposite: Spring cabbage Peter F1 from seed sown in August, over-wintered outside and harvested in the last week in April.

leaves and transplant spring cabbages out at 25-30cm apart, or closer if you intend to harvest alternate plants as greens, and leave the others to heart up. Plant winter cabbages out at 45-60cm to get good-sized hearts and keep the air moving between them. Remember to place the seed leaves level with the soil, water them in and press the soil very firmly around the roots.

Care

Put protection up immediately to keep out white butterflies, birds and rabbits. Cabbage root fly can be minimised by using collars (see general advice books) and if you spot yellowing leaves and weakened plants early on, lift the plants and crush the maggots to keep population numbers low. Cutworms (moth caterpillars) and leatherjackets (daddy-long-legs larvae) will eat roots and cut the plant off under the soil so if you see transplants wilt and fall over, sift the soil with your fingers until you find the culprit. Flea beetle can be irritating but this is rarely serious. Cover small plants with fleece if this bothers you and this will keep the root fly at bay as well. Mealy aphids can be picked or washed off and destroyed if you spot them early on and the plant will usually recover. Slugs and snails can be deterred while the plant is young by a variety of methods. I use the organically approved pellets from the Organic Garden Catalogue but these are only necessary until the plant gets large enough to cope.

I have had all the above problems but, thank goodness, I have not experienced clubroot which, I believe, is the worst disease of brassicas there is. I have seen the effects on an allotment in Scotland and it was horrible. However, there is loads of advice about how to minimise the effects

and get a decent crop. Meanwhile prevention, by paying careful attention to alkalinity and rotation, is all I can recommend. Keep cabbages well weeded and hoed.

Harvest

The idea for the hungry gap is to harvest the last of the winter cabbages in March and then the over-wintered spring cabbages in April and May. Some suggest that if you cut the cabbage and make a cross in the stem, fresh shoots that form small hearts will appear and make a small secondary harvest.

Afterword

Cabbages are heavy feeders so the onions that follow them need compost or a light dressing of manure to do well. The type of allium that goes in depends upon when the cabbages have been harvested. Leeks, over-wintering onion sets or garlic are all possibilities. After the spring cabbages come out and before garlic goes in (around the beginning of October), there is the opportunity for a green manure crop of mustard which could be dug in, and which is consistent with the brassica rotation. Alternatively a crop of leafy spinach could be harvested and/or dug in.

Opposite top: Delaway loose-leaved spring cabbage. Middle: January King photographed in March. Bottom: Red cabbage sprouting. The shoots and the heart of the cabbage are both tasty. Photographed on the 18th April, it is unusual for a red cabbage to stand for so long.

Carrots

Daucus carota

Carrots come in all colours these days and can make a real splash on the plate. We eat these raw as sticks or grated in salad. Combined with seeds, nuts and cabbage they are sweet and juicy. On their own steamed or, in casseroles to add colour and sweetness, they are one of the essential vegetables. For a treat cook small carrots whole with a little water and a knob of butter in a pot with a tight lid until they are just soft, the liquid is absorbed, and they are lightly glazed. The larger ones roast well. A glut, should you be truly fortunate, can be juiced or made into wine. There is no need to peel organically grown carrots.

Rotation
Roots.

Soil
A light soil to which no additional manure or compost is added is best. Remember onions precede them in the rotation. Carrots will benefit from a liquid comfrey feed as they grow.

Situation
My carrots are grown in several different situations on my plot. Most are in the sun under fleece. Some are under fleece in the shade tunnel where they don't grow quite as fast but can reach a good size. Some are sown very late (October, November and February) under fleece in the polytunnel or greenhouse where they provide small pickings for the hungry gap months.

Varieties
Nantes and Amsterdam Forcing sown late (see above) provide small carrots in March, April and May. The following are sown earlier and grow larger. Chantenay Red-Cored, lasts well in the ground, although Autumn King is recommended by most for winter growing. Two varieties supplied by Real Seeds (Resources; p.149), 'Giant Red' and 'Jaune Obtuse de Doubs' (an attractive yellow carrot) have also done well. I have yet to try 'Lisse de Meaux' which is recommended as a good keeper. Manchester Table, a heritage variety, makes large roots and stores well in horticultural sand until spring.

Sow
I sow large carrots for the hungry gap in July. Prepare the ground well. Fork it deeply. If you have heavy soil, build the bed upwards with leaf mould, sand and compost to give a good root run. Mark rows east to west across the bed. Make drills 2cm deep with rows 30cm apart. Sow thinly and cover. If the ground is very dry, water the drills before sowing.

Plant
I wouldn't recommend transplanting module-sown carrots. I have used root trainers to bulk up seed. It is tricky to handle the tiny seedlings without damaging the fine straight roots that are so desirable in carrots, and the resulting plants although large, have been slightly contorted. It was however successful. Storing them over winter and planting them out the following spring resulted in a good crop of seed. This method is too expensive and labour intensive for other than this purpose. If you have the room and wish to save seed from your favourite variety it is simpler just to let the crop over-winter in the ground.

Above: Sowing carrots at the end of July (1-5). I have lifted, dried off and stored the onions that were in this bed. I forked and raked the soil to remove large stones and hammered stakes in on the left to mark the end of each row. Note the extra stake at the end to give the first (and last) rows a bit of space. I pushed my trusty planting stick into the soil to make drills and sowed the seed thinly along the rows. Next I put opposing stakes and glass jars in place and covered the bed with fleece. This was then weighted down by metal bars and planks of wood I have collected for this purpose. The last image (6) shows roots I have pulled from the last rows seven months later on a frosty morning in March.

Care

There are several steps in the care of carrots to ensure good roots.

The first is protection against carrot fly. Some say that timing is crucial: if you plant after the life-cycle of the fly then you won't be infested. Some say that sowing thinly enough not to have to thin doesn't release the odour that attracts the fly. There are also carrot fly resistant varieties on the market. I haven't yet been successful with these measures. There are also non-organic methods but I've ruled those out. My method is illustrated here. Although this appears to be a lot of trouble, I now grow consistently good carrots. An improvement would be to use a heavier weight mesh but it is more than twice the price of fleece.

The second thing to pay attention to is to protect the newly germinated seedlings against slugs. It is possible to think that your carrots haven't germinated at all when in reality they have come and gone and you've missed it. On days 13 to 15 after setting your seed get out the organic slug pellets (beer-traps, torch and scissors – whatever your preferred method) and attack. Once the seedlings get 4-5cm high they no longer seem to be as attractive to slugs, so it is seldom necessary to repeat this procedure. An exception to this is that slugs will sometimes eat away the tops of mature carrot roots. Earthing them up helps with this and also prevents the tops turning green. I have had creatures with small sharp teeth (mice?) eat the tops of the roots and earthing up also helped with this.

The third is that if you don't thin your carrots you won't get large roots. I make two thinnings. Once when the seedlings are still tiny to about 2cm between each plant and the next time when the thinnings are baby-carrot size and we can eat them, to about 5-8cm between plants.

The fourth thing you must do is to keep the carrots weeded until they are sufficiently large to out-compete any weeds and if they are tucked away under fleece it is tempting to ignore this.

After all this you will never take a carrot for granted again!

Harvest

Yes!! Loosen the soil alongside the rows with a fork before lovingly sliding out the beautiful roots. Fill in the holes with soil to restrict access by pests. Harvest the roots as you need them or lift them to store in the autumn before the first frosts. Layered, not touching, in sand or used compost, they need to be somewhere rodent-proof. We keep a bucket of used compost at home in the cool so that a few days-worth can be lifted and kept at any one time. It keeps them to perfection.

Afterword

Plant the cleared bed with green manure (phaecelia or rye) or pile on the well-rotted manure or compost in readiness for next year's potatoes.

Opposite: Manchester Table carrot flowering in July.

Cauliflower

Brassica oleraceae Botrytis Group

Raw, or in curries are favourite ways to eat cauliflower and we do like cauliflower cheese.

Rotation
Brassica.
Soil
Medium rich and firm.
Situation
Sunny.
Varieties
Variety is the key when planning your time of harvest. Seed companies identify winter and spring harvesting cauliflowers clearly. I have had good results with Winter Walcheren types and the purple-curded Purple Cape. From a May sowing the heritage variety St George will crop at the end of March.
Sow
In March to May (May is better) set seed in a 9cm pot or a tray outside in an open cold frame or in a seedbed protected from birds and rabbits.
Plant
Prick out young seedlings when they are large enough to handle into modules or into 6-7cm deep multi-purpose compost. Grow them on until they have 4-5 proper leaves and are about 10-12cm tall. Plant them out into a bed that has been manured in the previous winter, forked over and trodden down firmly. Make holes with a dibber, trowel or bulb planter 70-80cm apart. Closer spacing yields smaller caulis. Set the young plants so that their seed leaves are level with the surface of the soil, water them in well and allow the water to drain away before firming the soil back around them. On my 110cm wide beds I plant one row of caulis down the middle and a row either side of summer cabbages. Once these are harvested the bed space is left to the caulis which can grow very large.
Care
Keep them hoed and well protected from all the usual brassica pests.
Harvest
Cauliflowers can be like busses and all come along at once. Breaking the leaves over the curds while they are still firm and before they start to break up prior to flowering, can help to keep them. The leaves immediately around the curd are very tasty.
Afterword
Prepare for onions or, if you have too much space allocated to onions, plant out a neutral summer crop such as lettuce. If this is out of the ground by July the bed could be used for over-wintering onions from seed.

Above: Cauli seedlings coming through.
Below: Intercropping with earlier maturing summer cabbages. The caulis are the middle row.

Celeriac

Apium graveolens var. rapaceum

Celeriac is a most rewarding crop to grow. It is delicious grated raw into cole-slaw. It can be cut into chunks and roasted or mashed on its own or combined with potatoes or carrots. Sliced finely and baked with cream and herbs in the oven it is fit for a dinner party.

Rotation
Roots.

Soil
Rich and well-drained.

Situation
Full sun. I have not been successful in partial shade.

Varieties
I have tried Prinz and Giant Prague and had success with both.

Sow
In February or early March on heat. Scatter a pinch of the very fine seeds as thinly as possible on the surface of multipurpose compost in a 9cm pot and cover lightly with compost. Keep the propagator covered night and day until the seeds germinate then remove the cover during the day so that the young seedlings don't get too stretched in the low light.

Plant
When the first true leaf appears, prick seedlings out into a tray about 5cm apart. I move trays into the green-house at this stage where it is cool at night. Grow the plants on until they are about 5cm tall and move to an outdoor cloche that is slightly venti-lated. You can open the cloche during the day and close at night if you want to but I don't bother as they are quite robust. Keep them well-watered. Transplant the plants when they fill the tray with their roots (check under-neath). Plant them out on a grid so that they occupy alternate spaces at a distance of about 30-40cm.

Care
Hoe regularly and water in dry spells. Celeriac likes lots of water. Go around each plant and remove the outermost leaves and any shoots that might be forming in between these leaves and the main root. The object is to create as smooth a root as possible. Celery leaf miner attacks the leaves occa-sionally and brown patches will ap-pear. Pick off the affected leaves and destroy them. Sometimes water will collect in the middle of the plant and start to rot the root. Eat those first.

Harvest
I leave celeriac in the ground until it is needed, digging them up so that the ones left are all down one end of the bed (see the note below on planting early potatoes). If you get heavy frosts it may be necessary to lift and hang them somewhere cool or pack them in used compost. They are large plants with an extensive root system. If you are storing them do your best to shake the soil from the roots but don't trim the roots away until you need to for the kitchen as the cut surfaces go an unattractive rusty grey.

Afterword
Celeriac is an unusual root in the rota-tion as it requires extensive feeding and the bed is still quite rich once the roots have been harvested. Potatoes go in next and will require rather less muck than they would after parsnips or carrots.

Opposite: Celeriac in the first week in May (after 14-15 months of growing).

Chard, perpetual spinach & wild seabeet

Beta vulgaris L.

Recipes from these versatile leafy greens can be as simple or as complex as you like. Small leaves can be used in salads and larger leaves as a steamed vegetable. They can be added to soups, packed with soft cheese in filo parcels or layered into lasagne. One of my favourite ways with chard is from my first culinary hero, the Galloping Gourmet. He stripped the green from the stalks and cooked it like spinach. The hard stems he chopped finely on the diagonal, combined them with onion, garlic, oil, herbs, and tomatoes (from the freezer or jars in the hungry gap) and served this as a separate dish. Both the soft greens and the sauce go well with pasta. The texture of wild beet cooked is surprisingly soft for such a dark green leathery-looking plant and the flavour is similar to spinach.

Rotation
These plants are members of the Chenopodiaceae and don't suffer from persistent soil-borne problems, so they can be neutral in the rotation. I include the chard and perpetual spinach with my roots however, as I like to keep track of where they have been.

Soil
Leafy beets do well on my sandy soil when it is poor to moderately rich, and I suspect they would do well in a wide range of soils.

Situation
They are tolerant of some shade.

Varieties
A wide range of chards are available in the catalogues and are easy to grow. I grow red or Rhubarb chard, yellow chard and white or Swiss chard, as well as a heritage green-stemmed variety that is slower to bolt than the others. Perpetual spinach readily self-seeds. Wild seabeet comes up in the seaweed I collect from the quay to spread round my asparagus and seakale. I let it grow where I want it and weed it out where I don't. Seabeet doesn't transplant.

Sow
You can sow direct in drills but I have more luck with spacing by setting the seed in a small pot outside and going from there. Sowings at the end of June or in July of chard and perpetual spinach over-winter well in my area.

Plant
Set the plants out about 30cm apart and water them in well.

Care
Keep them well hoed and remove outer leaves that start to decay. Chard can suffer from mildew which generally means that the roots are dry.

Harvest
Pick the outermost leaves first and the plant produces more. As the plant starts to bolt keep harvesting until the leaves become bitter.

Afterword
Dig the plants up and chop the large roots a bit before putting them on the compost heap. Summer crops like lettuces, neutral in the rotation, generally follow at this point to give the ground a bit of a rest.

Opposite: Yellow chard photographed in mid-April.

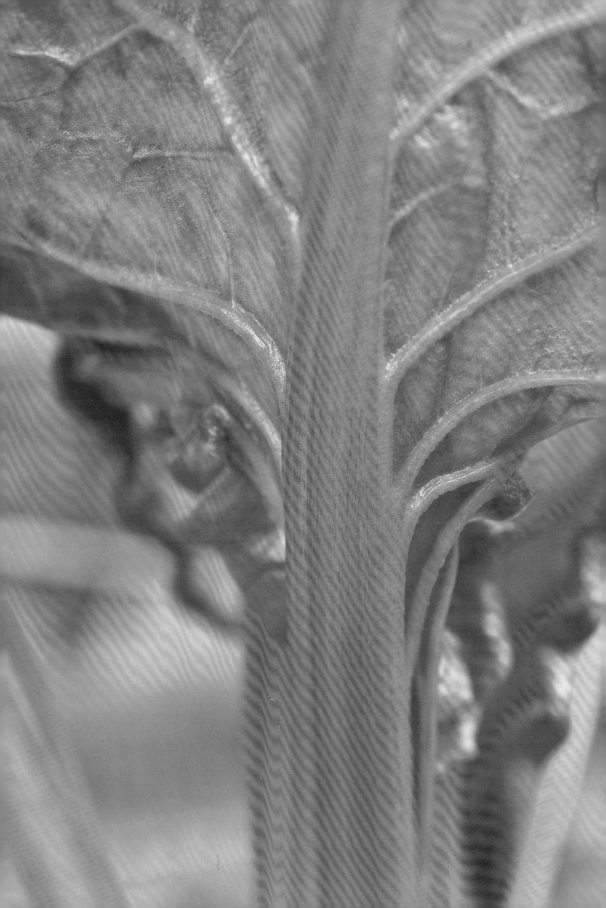

Above: Perpetual spinach in mid-April, just about to bolt.
Below: Seabeet self-seeded to the side of the seakale bed. Photographed in late March.

Chicory & Endive

Cichorium intybus L. & Cichorium endivia L. Scarole

I rely on these closely related leafy vegetables year on year to provide large amounts of slightly bitter leaves for mixed salad. If you like bitter Italian vegetables then these are a 'must have'. Shredded and stir-fried then the bitterness lessens and suits those less generally pleased with endive and chicory flavours. Since I discovered 'Pain de Sucre' (sugar-loaf chicory) I no longer bother with forcing Witloof roots. One year I did so and started a greenfly farm in the shed. I find the outdoor type much more trouble-free. Red chicories and endives are also easy to grow and good value in the spring.

Rotation
Neutral.

Soil
Poor to medium rich.

Situation
Sunny.

Varieties
Chicories I have tried are 'Pain de Sucre' or 'Pain di Zucchero' (pale yellowy green), 'Rossa de Treviso' (attractive pink-red pointed loose-leaves that go pale when blanched) and Pallo Rossa (forms hearts). Endives are Scarole Jeti, a large flat-leaved endive and the curly-leaved, yellow-green Bianca Riccia da Taglio. There are many varieties of chicories and endives available, especially from Italian seed companies.

Sow
June to August and later under cover for a spring harvest. I sow mine in small rows across a seed tray or in 9cm pots outside in an open cloche but they can be sown direct and some (e.g. Raddichio) may be better direct.

Plant
Prick seedlings out 5cm apart into trays to let them grow on until they make robust small plants with good root systems (check bottom of the tray). Plant out into beds 20-30cm each way. Water, let the water drain and firm the soil in around the roots.

Care
Hoe and hand weed if necessary between the plants. The only problem I've encountered is when I sow too early, and the plants bolt prematurely. Sometimes there is a bit of tip burn on the leaves which is due to a calcium deficiency, so applying calcified seaweed would fix that if it became a major problem.

Harvest
Let them stand and pick them as needed. 'Pain de Sucre' can cope with a light frost. The outside leaves turn brown and sometimes slimy, but inside there is usually a tightly wrapped self-blanched jewel the size of a pointed cabbage. If you catch them at the time when this outer covering is papery, they will store for longer than a month in a cool shed. Raddichio will stand frost and light snow, turning a brilliant red in the cold. Endives are easily blanched prior to harvest by covering them with a pot or a plate.

Afterword
Pick up the rotation from what was planted before the chicories and treat the bed accordingly. For example don't add anything if setting carrots, add manure if planting potatoes.

Top left: Bianca Riccia da Taglio at the end of April.

Top right: Pain de Sucre in the shade tunnel at the beginning of March.

Above: Red chicory in late March.

Opposite: A leaf from inside Pain de Sucre.

Garlic

Allium sativum L.

If you like garlic then you probably like it in almost everything. Every October I plant around fifty cloves of the ordinary bulb type for us and we almost always run out. We also like 'elephant' garlic which is milder and wonderful roasted. It is said to be related to the leek. Both types are relatively easy to grow.

Rotation
Onion.

Soil
Both types do well on my sandy soil over chalk with plenty of well-rotted manure incorporated at the roots.

Situation
Sunny.

Varieties
Any bulb type that is recommended for winter planting. I save my own cloves every second year and buy in named and certified virus-free stock otherwise. One year I got a good crop from some I bought in the market but this is a risky practice (see the note on white rot below). I save my own cloves of 'elephant' garlic as it usually looks healthier than what I've been able to obtain from suppliers, but you will have to start somewhere.

Sow
Not from seed.

Plant
Both types go in during October. Plant cloves of bulb garlic with the basal plate down about 10cm deep and 15-18cm apart with 30cm between rows. Plant 'elephant' garlic cloves basal plate down into 16cm deep holes 25cm apart with 30cm between rows. With 'elephant' garlic a bulb planter really comes into its own. The rows should be wide enough to get a hoe through without nicking the stems.

Care
Keep well-weeded to avoid competition and give a liquid feed towards the end of February and again in April as this makes a big difference to the yield. Pick off the seed heads as they form. If the spring and early summer are dry keep them well-watered. Rabbits like the young shoots so if this is a problem, drape the beds loosely with chicken wire. Garlic can be badly affected by white rot. Prevention is possible by keeping strictly to the rotation and never adding garlic or onion waste to the compost heap. If you have it then keeping the ground free of all alliums for eight years is recommended.

Harvest
Usually some time in June, after most of the leaves have gone yellow, the bulb garlic is ready for lifting. Lay the bulbs out on a rack in the sun to ripen for 2-3 weeks. They will stand a shower of rain but bring them under cover to avoid a real soaking. Once properly dry the outer leaves can be rustled off and the roots trimmed. Tie them in bunches and store them somewhere light and airy and not too warm. Get the conditions right and they will last right through to the middle of April. It is of course possible to harvest the roots early to use as wet garlic if necessary. The 'elephant' garlic lasts rather longer in the ground and is dried in the same way. The large cloves of this type rarely last as long as they get eaten, but they will last if that is what you want.

Opposite: Garlic photographed in mid-February.

Afterword

I usually set carrots after garlic so nothing needs to be added to the bed. A July planting of carrots will go in almost straight away. Hoe to keep the bed free of weeds. Lay down some bits of old board and you will be able to pick slugs off when they congregate under them.

Below: Elephant garlic, autumn-planted bulb garlic, and maincrop onions after lifting at the end of July. They all keep well for the hungry gap.

Opposite: The strong tops of elephant garlic in April. The leaves look similar to leek leaves.

Kale

Brassica oleracea Acephala Group

Kale is good for you and, as the other members of my family love it, I grow it. Not so secretly I only have time for two types cooked. 'Black Kale' is excellent wilted and stirred through beans and ham and pasta or in soup. 'Asparagus Kale', where the young shoots are harvested and eaten in a way similar to purple-sprouting broccoli, is delicious. The side shoots of 'Raggedy Jack' and the very similar 'Russian Kale' are delicious eaten raw.

Rotation
Brassica.

Soil
Poor to medium rich. Well drained.

Situation
They will stand some shade. 'Raggedy Jack' did very well for me one year on the north side of my polytunnel.

Varieties
'Cavalo Nero', sometimes known as 'Black Kale' and very similar to 'Nero di Toscana'; 'Raggedy Jack' and similar varieties such as 'Red Winter' and 'Russian Kale'; the heritage variety 'Asparagus Kale'. These are the ones I would recommend, but a lot of people grow curly green and red kales and they are very pleased to do so. Experiment and find out what you like. Growing conditions are similar for all with allowances made for varieties that grow very large.

Sow
Sow the seeds in April and May either in a seedbed, or in a 9cm pot of multipurpose compost outside.

Plant
Prick out the seedlings when they are large enough to handle into a tray of compost making sure there is at least 5cm between the plants. Grow them on until they have 4-5 true leaves and plant them out 30-60cm apart depending upon the variety. Water them in well, let the water drain and firm the soil well in around the roots.

Care
Hoe around the plants regularly and give the taller varieties some support as they risk being blown over in the wind. Some protection from white butterflies is good. Protection from birds is sometimes necessary and, although they are not pigeons' preferred snack, I have seen 'Cavalo Nero' plants stripped by them in early spring. Grey and white aphids can also attack the young leaves. Pick or wash them off; the plants usually recover.

Harvest
Single leaves can be harvested at any time. If you pick from the centre of 'Black Kale' plants the side shoots that come in February to May are tender. The flower buds are also delicious steamed or added to salad.

Afterword
Onions follow brassicas and by the time the kale plants are finished the leeks need planting out. A moderate amount of well-rotted manure is needed for decent-sized leeks. Alternatively, if you want to rest the ground, broadcast a green manure of mustard which is compatible with the rotation. Dig this in when it is 15-20cm high, leave for a month, and set out over-wintering onion sets in August or September for use at the end of spring the following year.

Opposite: Kale in November.

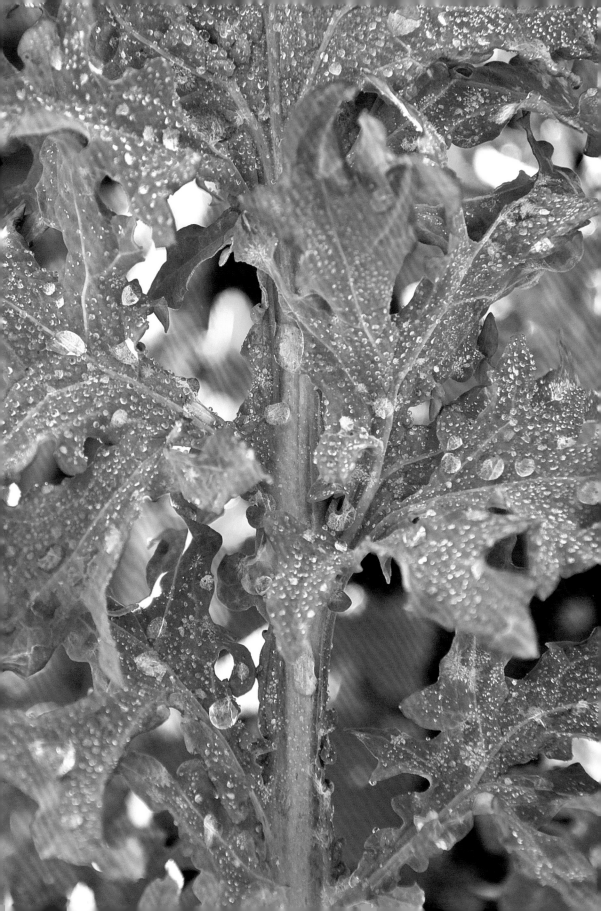

Leeks

Allium porrum

These come into their own in the hungry gap and they can be truly luxurious if their white shank only is braised and served with a sauce. I love the layers with their translucent white and pale yellow colours. The tops sliced finely make delicious soups. They are one of the easiest vegetables to grow.

Rotation
Onion.
Soil
Medium rich and well-drained.
Situation
Sunny.
Varieties
Choose a variety that will stand until the end of April. 'St. Victor' which has attractive blue/purple leaves does well for me as does 'Bleu de Solaise'. 'Atlanta' is another one that does well in the cold and 'Musselburgh' is a favourite for its reliability.
Sow
In a seedbed in March or April. Prepare the soil by raking it well, and draw out drills 2cm deep and 15-20cm apart. Place the seed as thinly as you can, ideally there should be a centimetre between each seed but this is difficult to manage. Leave them to grow on until they are pencil thick.
Plant
Make sure the bed is well-prepared with the soil forked over and well-rotted manure is incorporated. If the bed is dry, then dibbing out leek holes can be frustrating as the earth around the edges crumbles back into the hole. A tip is to water the surface of the soil so the holes will stay firm. Make the dibber holes 15-20cm deep or deeper if your seedlings are taller than this. Place holes about 20cm apart with 25cm between rows. Lift the young plants gently from their seedbed and drop them one at a time down into

the centre of each hole. Sometimes I trim the roots to within 3cm of the base of the young plant, but this is not necessary for anything other than ease of planting. Some people also trim the leaves. Fill the hole with water from a can without a rose. There is no need to fill the hole in with soil.
Care
Keep the bed weed-free by hoeing regularly between and hand-weeding within rows. Leeks can suffer from rust and while this doesn't seem to do much harm, I wouldn't save seeds from infected plants as it can pass on through the seeds. There are some common weeds that serve as hosts for rust. I often see it on Groundsel, for example. I try hard to eliminate this from the plot but it is persistent.
Harvest
Dig them as required and if you need the bed for anything or snow is forecast, heel in the last few somewhere handy.
Afterword
My hungry gap leeks are out by early May. I don't add anything to the bed at this stage if I'm growing parsnips or maincrop carrots.

Opposite: Leek seedhead from a variety that matured in the autumn photographed in the third week in May.

Over: Leeks from a late-maturing variety harvested on 1st May. Variety is the key to having leeks when you want them.

Lettuce

Lactuca sativa

I am astonished that more people don't grow lettuces throughout the winter as they do so well. Some varieties will bounce back from frost and snow and just keep growing very slowly until they put on a spurt in spring. Give them a little cover and their growth is lush. We eat more lettuce combined with other leaves in the winter and hungry gap months than we do in the summer. It is the perfect accompaniment to a pasta meal with tomato sauce and basil pesto from the freezer, and takes very little time to prepare.

Rotation
Neutral. However, move them around as they can get root aphids.

Soil
They tolerate a wide range of fertility. Not too rich for winter lettuces as they tend to get botrytis (a fungus; the leaves turn yellow and wilt).This is a particular problem under cover where the watering is tricky to get right.

Situation
Full sun and sheltered from the wind.

Varieties
Variety is the key to success with winter lettuce. I grow Winter Crop, Winter Marvel, Winter Density, and Lattughino. Lattughino is a fantastic lettuce and grows well outside and under cover.

Sow
A pinch of seeds in a 9cm pot of multipurpose compost in August will give you lettuces for outside, and later than this will refresh supplies for the polytunnel and greenhouse.

Plant
Prick out seedlings into trays to grow them on. When they have developed good roots and a few small leaves set them out in the beds 20-30cm apart depending on the variety. Air around them under cover is essential and they are more productive if they have a large root run.

Care
Keeping them weeded is less of a problem in the winter than it is for summer lettuces as the weeds grow very slowly. Keeping the soil hoed deters slugs and snails.

Harvest
Either whole or leaf by leaf. Lattughino does particularly well leaf by leaf. Removing the ones nearest the soil discourages slugs, and the plant goes on all winter generating fresh leaves from the centre before finally sending up a flower stalk.

Afterword
Refer to the crop before the lettuces were planted and go back into the rotation. It is wherever you got up to in your plan that counts. Sometimes I give the soil a rest with a planting of green manure: mustard will fit into a brassica rotation, red clover into legumes and Hungarian rye and phaecelia are neutral.

Above: Lattughino outside in April.
Opposite: Lettuces in March in the polytunnel.

Onions & Shallots

Allium cepa & Allium cepa Aggregatum Group

Surprisingly, not everyone eats onions and I imagine this makes their life quite difficult as onions may be added to practically every savoury dish. They are included in stocks, soups, curries, casseroles, sauces and stir-fries. The list is endless. We find it essential to have a good supply stored up for the winter and I have experimented with different types of onion to have them fresh through-out the winter and spring.

Rotation
Onion.

Soil
Moderately rich.

Situation
Full sun to do well.

Varieties
I grow several different types of on-ion. The easiest maincrop bulb onions to grow are white onions from sets. Jet Set and Sturon both do well for me. Red Baron from sets is a tasty red onion that sometimes keeps until the spring. I am particularly fond of a red onion called Red Brunswick. I keep the seed going from an original sam-ple from the HSL by planting mature bulbs in the spring, and collecting the seed to plant the following year. One tip for fresh onions in spring is to find a supplier that does generous packets of seed for large onions (Resources; p.149), and sow the seeds thickly in late summer under cover (this works in my 'shade' tunnel and the poly-tunnel) for larger than usual 'spring' onions in March. Then there is the Welsh onion. Happy to grow outside all year, reproducing itself by bunch-ing and sending up seed heads that germinate and extend your patch, this onion is fantastic in spring. I grow Longor shallots. I like the shape and flavour and they do consistently well in my situation.

Sow
If you are being careful with seed then sprinkle some into a 9cm pot and start them off in a propagator. The earlier in the year you start maincrop onions (January), the bigger they will grow. If sowing maincrop onions direct, wait until the soil warms up in March or April and thin them eventu-ally to 15cm apart. If growing pickling onions set the seed in April. If you are setting seed for 'spring' onions as above, make drills 2cm deep and sow under cover in September or October. Cover the seeds with soil and firm down the rows with the back of a rake.

Plant
Bulb onion seed set in small pots is grown on and pricked out into trays or modules before transplanting. The distances are as for sets. When plant-ing sets in March make sure that the bed is not too soft or too hard. After forking in compost or well-rotted manure I firm the soil down with the end of a rake and this seems to work fine. Sets are planted with their tips extending just above the soil, about 15-18cm away from each other, with 20-25cm between rows. Take care

Opposite top: Seedlings towards the end of March.
Middle: Bulb onion sets and shallots wait in my shed to be planted out early in March.
Bottom: 'Spring' onions that are really bulb onions harvested from the polytunnel in late April.

not to squeeze the sets as you push them into the soil as the growing tips are in there and you don't want to damage them. If the soil is too hard to push the set in easily, make a small hole first with your finger or a small dibber. Welsh onions can be propagated by lifting clumps in the spring, dividing them and replanting. Shallots can be started off in pots under cover in February or pushed into the ground outside a little later as for bulb onion sets but more widely spaced.

Care

Hoeing between the rows and weeding within them is essential to maintain a weed-free bed. In addition to suffering badly from competition, onions are sensitive to day length and will be affected by the shade from weed cover. If you see misshapen plants pull them out and destroy them. This is likely to be due to onion fly or eelworm. Onions are also susceptible to a number of fungal diseases. Attention to watering (don't overwater), practising good hygiene (don't put any onion waste on the compost heap) and sticking to the rotation should help with any problems.

Harvest

Maincrop onions are ready when the leaves turn yellow and fall over. This is anywhere from the end of June to the beginning of August. Loosen the soil under the roots with a fork and lay them out to dry off. I usually leave them on the bed for a few days and transfer them to a wire rack a few inches off the ground. After a couple of weeks the outside skins can be rustled off and the bulbs brought under cover. Sometime later they are plaited or strung and hung under cover in the front of my shed which is light, dry and cool. Any that are split at the base or have thick necks won't keep well, so use these first.

Afterword

Roots will follow onions so if you intend to plant carrots, parsnips or beetroot, set the bed with green manure (phaecelia or rye) to maintain the structure of the soil. Wait at least a month after digging the green manure in before sowing seed, as the ethylene produced by the decaying plants inhibits germination. If you intend to plant celeriac, pile on the manure and let the bed over-winter this way.

Above: Shallots in pots under cover in mid-March.
Below: Spring onions that have turned themselves into pickling onions photographed at the end of August.

Opposite: Shallots drying at the end of July.

Parsnips

Pastinaca sativa

A well-grown canker-free parsnip is, to me, a thing of great beauty. Roast or mashed, in soup or curry, sliced finely and deep-fried as crisps, parsnips are always welcome at our table. Parsnip wine is very fine. Parsnips don't need lifting and storing where I live so once they are in the ground and the young seedlings are growing away, the crop requires very little effort to maintain.

Rotation
Roots.

Soil
Deeply cultivated, well drained and not rich.

Situation
Sun or light shade.

Varieties
Tender and True has done consistently well for me. Gladiator F1 has also done well and both have some resistance to canker. Grow a short variety (e.g. Avonresister) if you cannot achieve the depth of soil necessary for long root growth.

Sow
I wait until April to sow as earlier has often been disappointing. Draw out 2cm deep drills (or press them out with a planting stick) and set three seeds together at 10-15cm intervals. Use fresh seed and do not be impatient for germination. One year I gave up after two months, hoed off the bed and set out squashes. The parsnips promptly germinated around the squash plants.

Plant
As parsnips from root trainers or modules are misshapen and small, it is better to sow the seed directly into the soil.

Care
It is essential to thin parsnips to one per sowing station. If you don't, the roots will be small. Celery leaf miner can be a problem. Squash the blisters or pick affected leaves off and destroy. Keep the crop weed-free and avoid damaging the roots when hoeing.

Harvest
Lift them as you need them. I find digging the soil away from the side of the parsnips allows the roots to be lifted without damage. If the soil freezes, you may need to store them in damp sand or used compost. Alternatively, heel them in somewhere sheltered and accessible. Dig a trench as deep as the length of your roots and lay the parsnips at an angle. Fill in with soil and leave the tops protruding. Heeling in slows down re-growth in the spring and is handy if you need the ground.

Afterword
Pile on the manure or compost once the bed is cleared ready for setting out potatoes in the spring.

Opposite: Tender and True parsnips harvested in March

Peas

Pisum sativum

These may seem out of place in a book about hungry gap vegetables but there are two ways they can be used. Dried peas are very tasty used instead of chickpeas in hummus. Soaked, boiled and blended with tahini, lemon juice, oil, herbs, seasoning and garlic we eat this as a dip or with winter salad leaves. The dried and soaked peas are also good cooked with ham and in soups and casseroles. The second use is as a supply of shoots to mix with salad. They are luxurious as a dressed fresh salad on their own. Mixed with the more gently flavoured lettuce and lamb's lettuce leaves available in the spring they add sweetness. In addition, mangetout will fruit early under cover if they are started in February.

Rotation
Legume.

Soil
Well drained and medium rich.

Situation
Sunny.

Varieties
I sow Gladstone, or some other heritage variety for drying. Old varieties usually give bigger peas than more recent introductions. Gladstone has advantages over others I have tried. It doesn't grow as tall (1-1.2m) as some others (e.g. Telephono or Magnum Bono, both of which yield well, need canes 1.8 to 2m long). It can be used as a dual purpose pea and is delicious eaten fresh. The pods ripen very neatly and predictably, filling at the base of the plant first, followed by the next node up and so on, which is an asset when picking. I use Telephono or just any pea seeds I have to hand for pea shoots. If you wish to freeze peas, the summer pea Greenshaft is good.

Sow
The Gladstone seeds are sown in February or March under cover. This is early to avoid the pea moth which can ruin the crop. I set the seeds 5cm apart in compost in guttering under cover. Homemade compost is good to use as the young pea shoots can be distinguished from any germinating weed seeds. The gutters are then perched on a structure that is impossible for mice to climb. Pea seeds for salad shoots are sown in shallow trays of compost at regular intervals to ensure a steady supply. They too need lifting away from the mice. Keep the germinating peas well-watered.

Above: Gutters are elevated to avoid mice. Photograph taken 18th April.

Opposite: Gladstone peas in early July.

80

Plant

Transplant your peas for drying to the bed when they are 8-10cm tall. Fork over the bed and scoop out two parallel trenches the depth of your gutters 60-70cm apart, oriented North to South along the length of the bed. Loosen the compost in the guttering by pushing the edges slightly towards the middle along the length of it. The roots of the young seedlings form a mat along the bottom of the gutter so the row binds together. The compost should be just moist for ease of handling. Place the end of the gutter furthest from you into the beginning of the trench, ease off the start of your row and jerk the guttering sharply once or twice, pulling the guttering out from underneath the seedlings as they settle into the row. This sounds tricky but it is quite easy to achieve. Water the young seedlings in well, allow the water to drain and firm the soil between and around them. At this stage the peas are no longer attractive to mice.

Erect climbing supports by inserting 1.5m canes at 30cm intervals at an angle to the outside of the newly planted rows and opposite each other, so that you make a long wigwam. I wire opposite canes together and stabilise the structure by resting poles along the top and wiring them to the others. Drape 10cm square plastic net over the canes. My peas don't have a hardening-off period and, if it is still quite cold when they are planted out, old fleece is draped outside the base of the canes. This serves several purposes. It keeps the wind off while the peas get used to being outside, it discourages birds and rabbits and it suppresses weed growth.

Care

Keep the rows reasonably well-weeded. I crop a row of lettuces down the middle of the row early on as the peas can stand a bit of competition. For pea shoots in trays under cover take care with the watering and feed at regular intervals with dilute liquid feed. The liquid that drains off my wormery diluted 1:5 with water is good for this purpose.

Harvest

We eat a few of the Gladstone peas fresh and this encourages the plants to fruit. The plants are then left until the foliage turns yellow, chopped off at the roots and stripped of pods, or they are hung intact under cover until I get time to deal with them. The timing of the harvest is reasonably critical and weather dependent. Rain followed by dry warmth can cause the mature pods to curl open and shed their fruit before you get to them. The pods are laid in a single layer somewhere warm and airy to finish drying. The shells are then removed and the seeds lie in a container with the lid off on a window sill for a while and finally, stored in airtight jars.

Pea shoots are harvested when the plants are 5-10cm tall. They will re-shoot again and again until they run to flower.

Afterword

Clear away the poles and netting from the beds and store under cover to use for the next year's crop. Hoe to remove weeds and mulch with a little well-rotted manure in readiness for brassicas (spring and other cabbages, or kale). If, however, you choose to grow oriental greens (many of which are brassicas) outside over the winter there should be no need to add extra feed prior to setting seed.

Opposite: Golden Sweet mangetout in mid-May.
Over left: Golden Sweet peas for use dried and as seed.

Over right: Peashoots flowering at the end of March after continuous cropping in the previous two months. The flowers are edible.

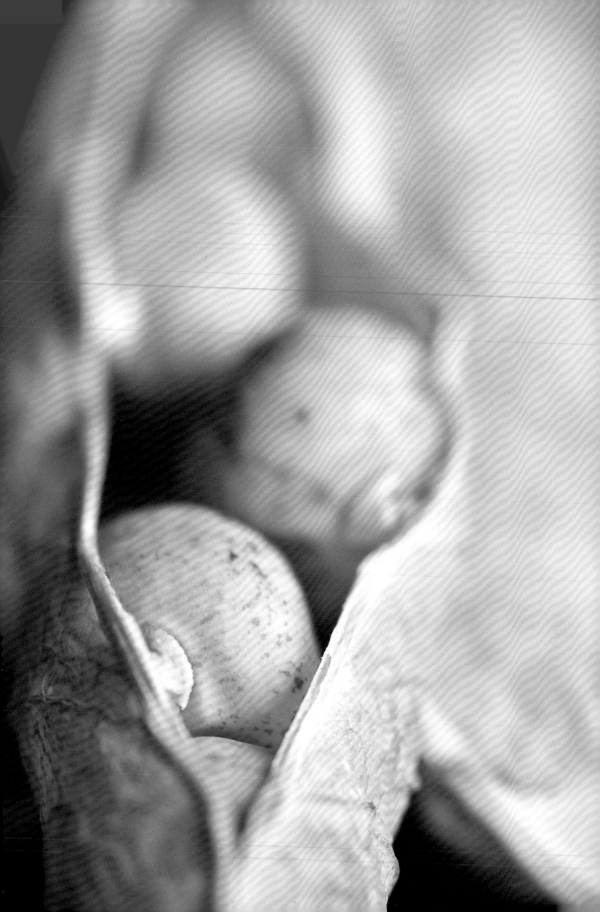

Potatoes

Solanum tuberosum

If you have limited space then you may decide not to grow maincrop potatoes, reserving your ground for more luxurious early and first early gourmet delights. However, finding a maincrop potato that will grow well (in my area this means resistant to blight), will store well and make a decent baking and roasting potato is more of an art than a science.

Rotation
Potato.

Soil
Rich and well-drained.

Situation
Sunny.

Varieties
Cara does reasonably well in Norfolk. Sarpo Mira and Sarpo Axona are the blight resistant varieties I grow to store. Tastier maincrop varieties such as Pink Fir Apple are always a disappointment for me. If you don't have a blight problem there is a fantastic range of great-tasting potatoes out there and the plant breeders are on the case these days with new ones appearing regularly in the catalogues. Learn by watching what does well for your neighbour.

Sow
Not from seed.

Plant
Although it is possible to save your own tubers it is not recommended, and certified virus-free stock is a safer way to go. Set tubers out to chit with the 'rose' end up in egg trays somewhere light and frost-free. Tubers of maincrop potatoes are planted in April when the chits or new shoots are 2-3cm long. The advice around here is that if you lower your trousers and can bear to rest your backside on the earth, then the soil has warmed up enough to put your spuds in. I've not seen anyone do this. Tubers are placed at the bottom of holes 15cm deep, right way up, and are spaced 60cm apart with 2 rows 60cm apart running the length of the bed. Initially the holes are filled level with the soil. I use my bulb planter to plant potatoes.

Care
As soon as the shoots appear, soil from between the rows is drawn up over the emerging shoots and straw mulch is heaped over them. This protects them from frost and stops the tubers that form near the surface turning green and unusable. This earthing-up will also demolish any weeds. Dense foliage from the plants soon makes weeding unnecessary.

Harvest
Ideally maincrop potatoes should be dug around the end of October. This has not in some years been achieved until as late as Christmas and the tubers have still kept well. It is likely, though, that the later you are with this task, the more damage there will be from slugs. Try to remove every last tuber from the bed, even tiny ones, as volunteers the following year harbour diseases and are a general nuisance.

Afterword
Autumn-sown broad beans can follow potatoes. Some of the beds can be planted with over-wintering lettuce before going back to the rotation the following spring with peas or beans. There is usually sufficient feed left after the spuds for any of these choices.

Opposite: A very fine chit in the third week of April.

Rhubarb

Rheum x hybridum

We eat rhubarb after it has been forced and when it is sweetest. It is great stewed gently with sugar or honey. Sweet cicely or angelica and ginger can be added for sweetness and flavour. Rhubarb crumble is a classic. Occasionally I will make a bulk harvest in May from unforced plants as it makes the most delicious wine. While I have met people who are sensitive to eating rhubarb, I have not yet met anyone who can't grow it.

Rotation
Permanent.

Soil
Rich.

Situation
It can stand a bit of shade but will do better in the sun.

Varieties
Early Champagne is said to be sweeter than most and is available as both sets and seeds. I think I have Stockbridge Cropper, but certainty is lost in the mists of time. All my plants come from one 'parent'.

Sow
I have not started rhubarb from seed and all the books seem to agree the results can be disappointing. If you want a named variety, buy in sets.

Plant
Most allotment sites have several long-lived plants and most allotment holders are only too willing to allow the removal of a shoot and root section (set) for transplantation any time between October and April. Let plants grow for four years before dividing them. Keep your sets moist if you can't plant them straight away. Dig holes deeper than you need 1-1.2m apart. Fill each with manure and mix this with the surrounding soil. I included a dusting of bonemeal with the ones I planted most recently and they have come away strongly. Re-make a hole for your set and water it in if the soil is dry. Cover the roots with soil and firm down leaving the bud uncovered.

Care
Keep weeded. Remove old leaves when the plant becomes dormant. Mulch well with manure and cut off flowering stalks when they come. I put my forcing tubs in place in January. Council compost bins are ideal for the purpose weighed down with a piece of board and a brick. A bit of light gets in but, more importantly, air does also and this helps to stop too many stems from rotting.

Harvest
Pull forced stems away from the edges of the crown. Grip them low down on the stalk to avoid breaking them. Remove the tub while some leaves remain and allow the plant to recover. Don't force the same plants two years in a row. Unforced plants can be harvested until the beginning of June. Eat only the stalk as the leaves are toxic. Put the leaves on the compost heap where the toxins can break down.

Afterword
Sometimes the plants rot from the middle and need regenerating. Start again with the outside buds and a piece of root somewhere fresh.

Opposite: Rhubarb stalk in the first week of April.

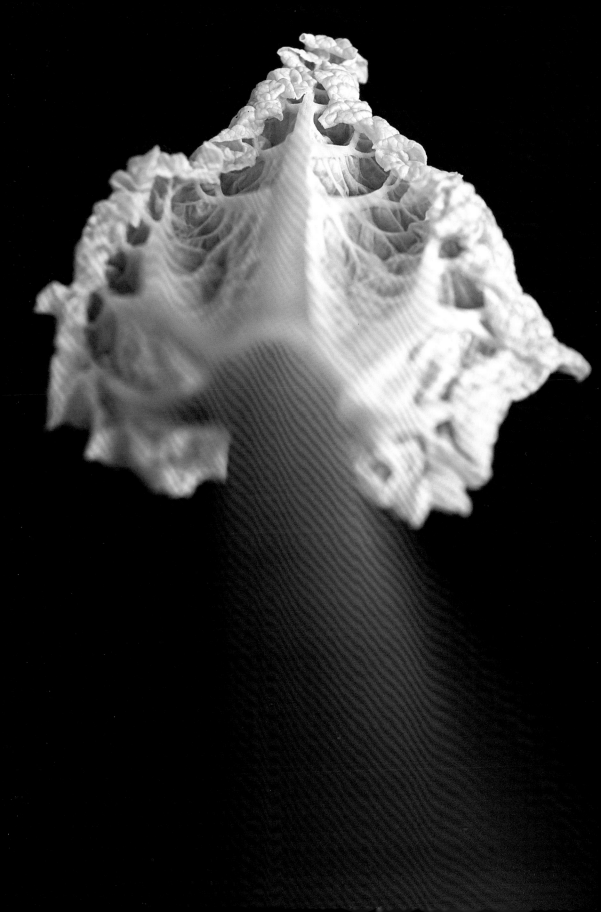

Salad leaves

These are the vegetables made popular in this country thanks largely to the efforts of Joy Larkcom. She has produced several excellent books on the subject (Resources; pps.144-145) and I do not do the topic justice here. We eat these mainly in salad and sometimes stir-fried. They make a spectacular healthy treat in the darker months of the year.

Rotation
As most of these are members of the cabbage family they go in the Brassica part of the rotation.

Soil
Medium to rich and well drained.

Situation
Sunny and sheltered outside or covered in fleece or green 'shade' netting. They also do well in the polytunnel or greenhouse.

Varieties
Rocket (salad and wild), Mizuna, Mibuna, Chinese Green-in-Snow, Red Mustard (two types: giant and frilly), Green Mustard (two types: giant and frilly), Golden Mustard, Tatsoi (rosette Pak Choi), Landcress, Lamb's Lettuce and Claytonia. This list is by no means comprehensive. Try salad mixes from the seed companies. Find ones that do well for you.

Sow
Directly into the soil in late summer and early autumn (July, August, September). A little later in the greenhouse or polytunnel will also give you a crop. Make drills 2.5cm deep with 30cm between rows. Space the seed very thinly along the row as individual plants will grow quite large (30cm or more across). Once you get Lamb's Lettuce to grow and self-seed you will never have to buy seed again and it will be a question of weeding out what you don't want.

Plant
There is no need to raise these in modules and some dislike being transplanted. That said, Mizuna and Tatsoi do well from modules as they are particularly resistant to bolting and, even if they do bolt, they can be encouraged to produce succulent side shoots for weeks.

Care
Keep them weeded and tidy yellowing leaves away from the bottom of the plants. If too many leaves go yellow, water with liquid feed either from the comfrey barrel or from the wormery. Keep plants in the polytunnel and greenhouse just moist.

Harvest
Cut rows with scissors about 5cm from the growing tips and the plants will re-grow. Pick individual leaves from larger plants for spicier flavours; pinch out any flowering shoots and side shoots will sprout for your later harvests. The flowers are colourful and tasty in salads.

Afterword
Clear the beds when cropping is over (the middle to end of spring) to make way for maincrop onions. Oriental greens and salad leaves are not heavy feeders like cabbages and cauliflower; some well-rotted manure or compost should be added to the beds before the onion sets go in.

Opposite from left to right, starting at the top: Rocket flowers (April); Tatsoi flowers (March); seedlings of Tatsoi, Wild Rocket and winter lettuce (late November for planting out in the tunnel); Landcress (late March); Tatsoi (late February); cut and come again Oriental Saladini (mid-March); Lamb's Lettuce (mid-March); Mibuna (late March); Mizuna and Red Mustard (late October); Wild Rocket seedlings (for planting out, late October).

Seakale

Crambe maritima

A native to the Southern UK coastline, seakale is a most delicious spring vegetable treat equal to asparagus and sprouting broccoli. It tastes a little like asparagus with cabbage and celery-like undertones. The golden spears steamed lightly and served with a knob of butter look impressive on the plate.

Rotation

Seakale is a brassica and may get brassica-type problems. They are grown in a permanent bed unless you have to move them if they get clubroot. Be certain when you plant seakale that it is where you want it to be. It is difficult to remove once established as severed roots deep in the soil continue to send up shoots that must be pulled for the next two years. If, for example, you decide to site a polytunnel over your seakale bed at some later date, then you may have a problem.

Soil

Deep, rich and sandy.

Situation

Sunny to do well.

Varieties

There is a pale green type that is very vigorous, and a red-tinged cultivar. Both are attractive and taste good.

Sow

I started my bed from seeds sown in a tray under cover in April. I grew them on in 9cm pots and later transplanted them 40cm apart (but see below). The seeds are covered in a corky layer that helps them float about the seashore so this needs scraping away to allow germination.

Plant

Plants can be moved but most usually, seakale is grown from root cuttings. Take cuttings by digging up a healthy plant in November. Choose pencil thick roots. Make a straight cut nearest the crown of the plant and an angled cut 10-12cm further away. One root can make more than one section. Remember to keep the end of the section that was nearest to the crown identifiable with a straight cut. Match ends together, make small bundles of six or so root pieces and tie them with raffia. Place the cuttings angled ends down in a tub of sand and cover. Buds will appear at the edges of the straight cut ends in spring. Prepare the new bed by adding manure and use a dibber to make holes as deep as the length of the root cutting plus 2.5cm. Plant the cuttings out when the buds are still very small (4-5 mm) and remove all but 3-4 of the new buds with a sharp knife. Drop the cutting into its hole and cover with soil.

The decision to re-site my seakale bed allowed me to revise my opinion on how far apart seakale should be planted. The plants can be very vigorous and do better with a generous spacing of 60cm. Clear the leaves away as the plants die down in the autumn and cover the plants with partially rotted leaf mould if you have it. Doing this warms them up and discourages slugs from eating the new shoots. Forced shoots are produced by covering the plant and its mound of leaves with a light-proof box or tub in December. Heaping fresh manure round the outside of the tub will also bring on the shoots but this is not necessary to get a good result.

Opposite: Seakale shoots coming through in March.

Care

Keep them well-weeded but take care not to dig too deeply around the plants, as cutting through the roots will encourage another plant to grow from any cuttings you made inadvertently. As the tubs are removed in the spring leave any manure used for forcing in place to feed the plants. Mulch the plants with seaweed if you can get it. Some gardeners force all plants every year but I have enough to force alternate ones. To keep the plants strong remove the pretty white flowers before they set seed.

Harvest

Lift your tub, brush away the plant's insulation and cut the pale shoots about 15cm long. Take 2-3 cuts from each plant (the vigour of your plant will determine the number of shoots you get). Remove the tub after this and allow it to recover.

Afterword

Yummy!

Above: Root cuttings prior to planting out in March.
Below: Seakale flowering at the end of May

Spinach

Spinachia oleracea L.

This is 'proper spinach' according to my family and is the preferred type of spinach in our household. We are conscious of 'making do' with chard or perpetual spinach. There is, however, a trade-off here as chard and perpetual spinach are much easier to grow. Steamed lightly or wilted in the pan with a knob of butter, spinach on its own is delicious. Leaves folded into pasta or through rice, or torn and added to salad are tasty and good for you. A suggestion for a special treat is to combine wilted leaves with soft cheese and bake them in filo pastry parcels. Spinach soup blended with cream, potato and garlic is another.

Rotation
Neutral, but I include them in the roots.

Soil
Moderately rich and moist.

Situation
Sunny.

Varieties
Almost any over-wintering variety will do well for you if you get the planting time right. I am trying a Giant type from Seeds of Italy at the moment and it is doing very well.

Sow
Outside in August and September. Make drills 2.5cm deep across the bed and set the seed about 8cm apart in rows 30cm apart. Draw in the soil to cover and firm down the rows with the back of a rake. Alternatively, broadcast seeds and rake them in.

Plant
Spinach does not do well transplanted from modules. (Note that chard and perpetual spinach will tolerate transplantation without bolting).

Care
Cover the bed loosely with netting to protect the young seedlings from pigeons. Hoe between the rows regularly. Pick off yellowing outer leaves. The plants continue to grow very slowly through the winter and do better with cloche protection but it is possible to get away without in my area.

Harvest
Pick outside leaves regularly to encourage new leaves to form from the centre. In the hungry gap months the plants put on a spurt and whole plants can be harvested. Pull them up and wash and trim off the roots.

Afterword
Spinach seed is expensive but it is easy to let a few plants (more than 16) go to seed. Choose an open-pollinated type to do this with as an F1 variety will not come true. Store whole dry plants upside down in a paper bag. Hang the bag away from mice as they love spinach seed. What you do to the bed next depends on whether you clear it after harvesting the spinach. If cleared, maincrop potatoes can follow so add well-rotted manure. If you allow the plants to stand, to harvest the seed, winter lettuce set out in September requires no additions.

Left: Plants harvested in April.

Squash

Cucurbita maxima

Roasted in chunks with the skin on or off, squash is a delicious accompaniment to other roasted vegetables and meat. Sliced more finely and baked with dried chillies, pine-nuts, sage, cinnamon and olive oil is a variation. We eat it in soups, curry, stews and sweet pies. A small amount mashed and added to the dough of scones or home-baked bread adds moisture. Pasta packets stuffed with herbs and mashed squash is another idea if you have the time.

Rotation
Neutral, but move them around as a precaution against disease.

Soil
Rich. One of my friends was particularly successful one year after planting them on her compost heap.

Situation
Sunny. Wind is a problem for squash plants so shelter is important.

Varieties
Choose your varieties according to flavour and keeping qualities. I have grown over the years, in order of preference, Uchiki Kuri, Crown Prince, Blue Ballet, Golden Hubbard, Butternut (C. moschata), Marina di Chioggia, Greenwich, Buttercup, Acorn (C. pepo) and Gem Store (C. pepo), trying a few different ones each year, looking for the squash with perfect keeping qualities. Out of these here Uchiki Kuri, Crown Prince, Golden Hubbard and Blue Ballet have stored the most successfully.

Sow
Set one seed per 9cm pot of multi-purpose compost in April, on heat if necessary. Place the seed on its side to lessen the likelihood of it rotting before germination.

Plant
Transfer the young seedlings to 2.5cm larger diameter pots to grow on for two to three weeks under cover. Harden them off gradually in a cold frame before planting them out at the end of May. If the cold weather persists, pot the young seedlings on into a pot the next size up before attempting to harden them off. Create low mounds of well-rotted manure mixed with soil 1-2m apart depending on whether or not your chosen variety is bush or trailing in habit and settle each plant into one of these. Water them in and firm the soil in well around the roots. Protect the tender young plants from slugs, snails and wind.

My allotment neighbour, who is better at squash than I am, sets her plants out under two litre plastic water bottles with the base cut off. She then inverts these and pushes them into the soil next to the plant to act as a water funnel later. Place a stick at least 60cm tall near the plant (or through the middle of the inverted water bottle) so that you know where to water if the season is very dry.

Care
Hoe the weeds as the plants establish. Squash plants grow quickly and the leaves are so large that continuous hoeing is not needed. Place the almost mature fruits on pieces of tile to keep them dry.

Harvest
To a large extent the weather will determine when you harvest. Wait until at least some of the leaves have

Opposite: Golden Hubbard in March.

died back. Cut a T-shaped 'handle' when removing the fruit from the plant. I don't ever use this as a handle though, as there is a risk of the stalk pulling off, in which case the fruit won't store. Support the weight of the fruit with both hands when you carry it and be careful not to bruise it. Set them somewhere on slats in the sun for 2-3 weeks to finish ripening and then bring them indoors. Be aware that they are very attractive to rats and mice. I have discovered that the ideal storage place for squash in our house is on the top shelf in our east-facing conservatory. I have tried the shed, greenhouse and a summerhouse but none of these were as successful. Check your fruits regularly for signs of rot.

Afterword

Move back into the rotation after clearing the vines away to the compost heap.

Top: Uchiki kuri in March.
Middle: Seedlings photographed in April.
Bottom: Crown Prince in March.
Opposite: Squash flower in July.

Turnip & Radish

Brassica campestris Rapifera Group & Raphanus sativa

Added to lamb stew or freshly grated into salad, turnip and radish can be very welcome during the hungry gap.

Rotation
Brassica (both).
Soil
Moderately rich.
Situation
Sunny, although they can stand a little shade.
Varieties
Turnips over-winter well in the polytunnel. The Giant Limousin turnip illustrated was photographed in March. Two sorts of radish are available for harvest during March, April and May: those that are sown in the late summer outside and over-wintered, such as Black Spanish Round, and those that are set under cover early in the season. These are the more well-known types that have short round red roots or longish red and white roots such as French Breakfast. Black Spanish Round can be eaten raw but is more usually cooked, with the faster-growing types eaten raw.
Sow
Turnips in the tunnel should be sown in September or October in drills 2cm deep with seed spaced 8-10cm apart. Seed can also be sown in modules. Set 2-3 seeds per module and transplant as a unit without disturbing the roots. I have found this method more successful when growth is rapid and turnips are planted outdoors in the spring for an early summer harvest. For radish that is over-wintered outside, the bed should be moderately firm and raked well. In July or August set the seed thinly in drills 1-2cm deep in rows 20-25cm apart. Thin to 10cm apart while the seedlings are still small. For radish early in the year under cover seed may be sown more thickly, or broadcast and raked in.
Plant
I have found the varieties mentioned here are more successful if sown direct.
Care
Keep them well hoed. Flea beetle can be a problem and you may have to cover late summer sowings with fleece to keep this irritating little creature at bay.
Harvest
Pull them as required. Cover them with straw if you think they may be damaged by frost, or lift and store in used compost.
Afterword
They are followed by onions, so a little well-rotted manure can be added to the beds.

Opposite above: Giant Limousin turnip grown to a moderate size under cover in the polytunnel.

Below: Black Spanish Round radish in March grown outside.

Rosemary flowers at the end of April.

Chapter 3
'hungry gap' herbs

Bay

I have found bay no trouble to grow and constantly useful in the kitchen. It adds depth of flavour to many savoury and some dessert dishes.

Rotation
Permanent.
Soil
Average.
Situation
Full sun and protected from the wind.
Varieties
Make sure you get the one used in cooking.
Sow
Difficult from seed.
Plant
The tree you see here was an offshoot and has developed offshoots of its own that I have not bothered to remove.
Care
Watch for scale insects which can be scraped off. I keep mine well cut back. Although it gets a bit of tip burn on the leaves it is no trouble for rich return.
Harvest
Any time.
Afterword
The leaves have a pleasing symmetrical shape and can make a base for chocolate leaf decorations for cakes.

Celery leaf

I started to grow leaf celery after frustrating experiences with celery. It is possible to use the leaf type as a substitute in many recipes. In stock or chopped fine in soups and salads it adds depth of flavour. It is tasty incorporated into potato rissoles or fishcakes and burgers. It is possible to grow celery leaf for nine months of the year, and as a hungry gap herb it is invaluable.

Rotation
I keep this in with the roots.
Soil
Medium rich and well-drained.
Situation
Sunny, although it can tolerate a bit of shade.
Varieties
Just the one.
Sow
In February, at the same time and in the same manner as celeriac.
Plant
Treat as for celeriac except for the planting distances in the beds. Set young celery leaf plants out more closely at 20-25cm apart.
Care
Celery leaf miner can be a bit of a pest. Pick the leaves off and squash the bug inside the blisters.
Harvest
Harvest single leaf stems or cut the whole plant off 2.5cm up from the base. Celery leaf puts on a growth spurt in the spring and it will grow a full crop again before eventually running to seed.
Afterword
Dig the plants up and consign them to the compost heap. Potatoes come next and will need more manure.

Opposite: My bay tree in March.

Chervil

I love the mild aniseed flavour of this herb. Together with parsley, chives and tarragon it has a reputation in French cooking as one of the 'fines herbes', a mix that is complementary to chicken, fish and egg dishes. Stirred through pasta with eggs and cream for example it is superb.

Rotation
Finally, I think I have been successful at establishing a 'naturalised' patch of this on my plot. It is separate from the rotation.

Soil
Moisture retention is more important than feed. Improve the soil with leaf mould.

Situation
An amount of shade is necessary for this herb. Provide some shelter in winter. The clump that has naturalised is sheltered from the north and east winds.

Varieties
The one that turns slightly purple in late summer (Anthriscus cerefolium).

Sow
Seeds are sown direct in spring (April) and in autumn (September).

Plant
Chervil does not like to be transplanted.

Care
Keep weeded and sheltered, both from the wind and direct sun.

Harvest
Cut when the fronds are 10-15cm tall.

Afterword
I'm still learning about this plant.

Chives

Chives are one of the first herbs to send out fresh shoots and they are at their best at this time. They are particularly good with eggs and cheese and often used as a garnish or in coleslaw to add a mild onion taste.

Rotation
Onion

Soil
Rich and moist to do well.

Situation
Sunny.

Varieties
I grow the purple-flowered variety.

Sow
Once you have a clump, chives readily self-seed. Otherwise sow the seed in March.

Plant
Create new clumps by dividing existing ones. Space clumps 15cm apart.

Care
Keep them well weeded. In certain locations some of mine have developed quite bad rust. The solution to this has been to dig up the clumps and take them to the green waste at the recycling centre where the temperatures are high enough to destroy the spores.

Harvest
Cut whole clumps to within 3cm of the ground and the clump will re-grow.

Afterword
It is important not to plant other alliums where chives have been.

Opposite: Chives in the polytunnel in April. There is very little time advantage to be gained from growing these under cover.

Dill

Dill comes earlier and can be started earlier than is often suggested on the seed packets. Small plants are available for harvest towards the end of the hungry gap. We enjoy this in potato salad and I love it with trout and sliced orange salad. The flowering head adds flavour to pickles and looks attractive. We save the seed and use it in bread and curries.

Rotation
If I wanted to start a new patch each year I would keep it in with the roots, but in practice I allow it to self-seed, and harvest or weed out the plants that are in the way.

Soil
It will handle a wide range of fertility and germinates on very poor patches.

Situation
Sunny.

Varieties
Just the one.

Sow
I started my patch from seeds sown in modules in February on heat. After this it has self-seeded annually. It is possible to have a crop in April from the greenhouse border.

Plant
Seedlings will transplant better from modules than trays as they don't like their roots disturbed.

Care
Keep it away from fennel as they can cross. Give the plants plenty of room as they may get greenfly if crammed together.

Harvest
Feathery leaves, decorative seed heads, seeds.

Afterword
It is interesting to let the dill come up where and when it chooses.

Fennel (herb)

We are not so fond of the strong taste of fennel and will use it only occasionally in a salad or with fish. The seeds add flavour to curry and make a refreshing tea.

Rotation
This herb will make very large permanent clumps if allowed. Bulb fennel, also known as Florence fennel, is kept with the roots rotation in the summer and autumn.

Soil
Well-drained and moderately fertile.

Situation
Partial shade.

Varieties
There are green and bronze types.

Sow
Direct in April or May, or sow into modules and transplant. The problem I have with herb fennel is removing it before it self-seeds.

Plant
Take care not to disturb the roots when transplanting. Fennel can be planted at single stations for effect in a border, especially bronze fennel which makes a very handsome large plant.

Care
Keep self-seeded plants well away from your dill.

Harvest
Leaves and seeds.

Afterword
It is a useful plant to have in the garden as it attracts hoverflies which help to control aphids.

Opposite: Fennel in April.

Lovage

This herb has a strong flavour and is, to my mind, much under-used. The new leaves in the hungry gap have a rich celery-like flavour so use it sparingly in salad. In vegetable stock, soups and sauces it serves to deepen other flavours. A favourite treat is a single leaf with mature cheddar in a sandwich.

Rotation
Permanent.
Soil
Medium rich and well drained.
Situation
Sunny.
Varieties
Just the one.
Sow
In May, in modules, under cover.
Plant
Transplant the seedlings when they are 6-8cm tall. Lovage will make large plants (up to 2m tall with a spread of 1m) so confine them to sunken pots if you wish to restrict their growth.
Care
Remove the flowering heads before they set seed.
Harvest
The small young leaves in the spring have the best flavour and are at their most tender.
Afterword
Make sure that it doesn't 'get away' and seed everywhere.

Marjoram

I have two types on the allotment. One has small green leaves with pinky-purple flowers and the other bright golden foliage. The first has a flavour that adds a pleasant earthy taste to dishes and goes particularly well with bacon and mushrooms. For preference I use the bright golden 'oregano' in tomato sauces.

Rotation
Permanent.
Soil
It will do well in quite poor but well-drained soil.
Situation
Sunny. A bit of shade will stop the golden type from scorching but also increases the green in the leaves.
Varieties
Several. Refer to Jekka's book to make your choices. If I was restricted to one I would choose the golden.
Sow
In May under cover. Seeds are available for a limited number of varieties.
Plant
Layers with roots form at the bottom of some varieties that can be detached and transplanted in August.
Care
Ensure that the plants don't take over more area than you want them to. Cut them back in November to within a few centimetres of the soil
Harvest
Harvest shoots with scissors when they are 10-15cm long and still soft. If you don't want to use all the shoots, trim the remainder off to keep the bush looking tidy and attractive. New shoots will soon reappear.
Afterword
Some varieties self-seed and spread..

Opposite: Lovage at the end of March.

Mint

As a tea, with new potatoes, in tabbouleh, with peas, in sauce – these are a few of the uses that spring instantly to mind when thinking of how we use mint. It is one of the most popular herbs. Fresh mint is far superior to dried mint so maintaining a continuous supply is important.

Rotation
Permanent. Move it if it becomes infected with rust.

Soil
Moderately rich and well-drained.

Situation
Will tolerate some shade.

Varieties
Several. Choose according to flavour. I have two mints. Their labels are long gone. The one I use for preference in cooking is green-leaved and strongly aromatic. The other is grey-leaved and hairy and always gets passed over for the kitchen. I keep it because it looks attractive and the butterflies like it.

Sow
Not from seed.

Plant
For use in the hungry gap plant up sections of root into pots of multipurpose compost in September. Place the pots in the front of an open cloche.

Care
Remember to water them.

Harvest
Cut the leafy stems regularly to prolong the harvest and prevent the plant from flowering

Afterword
Keep mint confined to a sunken pot otherwise it will spread everywhere.

Parsley

We use more parsley than any other herb. Chopped finely and added late to almost any dish – mashed potatoes, stir-fries, salads, casseroles – it adds flavour and colour and is an invaluable source of vitamins, iron and other minerals.

Rotation
I keep this in with the roots.

Soil
Moderately rich and well-drained.

Situation
Sunny if you want it to over-winter.

Varieties
I grow two types, Moss-curled and Flat-leafed. The curly parsley is in general more popular but the flat-leaved is an excellent substitute for coriander in salsa.

Sow
I sow seeds in a pot or tray on heat in February.

Plant
Transfer young seedlings to modules (one per module) and grow them on in the greenhouse. At 5-6cm tall they are hardened off. Plant 20cm apart.

Care
I have tried over-wintering parsley in the greenhouse but they became infested with greenfly and outside plants were only a few days behind. Liquid feed if leaves turn yellow. Pinch out flowering shoots.

Harvest
Picking the outside leaves first keeps the plants neat.

Afterword
Re-integrate the bed into the area for maincrop potatoes or plant lettuces.

Opposite: Mint early in March.

Poppy (breadseed)

I love to grow my own breadseeds for use in baking. Unlike ornamental varieties the seedheads hang on to their seeds and are harvested by turning the seedhead upside down. The plants are a talking point on the plot (yes, they are the same as the opium poppy, but it doesn't get hot enough here to develop the active ingredients, and the seeds contain no traces).

Rotation
Not part of the rotation and not permanent either.
Soil
Any.
Situation
Sunny to do well.
Varieties
I bought seeds to start with but the company no longer exists.
Sow
Allow some to spill as you harvest the pods in July. You could try germinating shop-bought breadseeds in May.
Plant
This may work. I've never had to try it.
Care
Thin them or you won't get big pods.
Harvest
As above.
Afterword
Hoe out unwanted plants as they tend to take over.

Rosemary

This is strongly flavoured and goes well with meat, lamb in particular.

Rotation
Permanent.
Soil
Well-drained and moderately fertile.
Situation
Sunny.
Varieties
Several. Choose according to growth habit as all types have highly aromatic leaves.
Sow
I haven't attempted this from seed.
Plant
Take softwood cuttings in March. Place 4 or 5 around the edge of a 9cm pot of free-draining compost and place in the propagator. Pot on into small pots, harden them off and set in their final places according to your purpose. If growing upright types as a hedge, place them 40-60cm apart. A friend of mine thinks this propagator business is an awful bother. He heels in cuttings and they just grow!
Care
Keep them well-trimmed for a continuous supply of fresh shoots. However, extensive cutting back in the autumn can lead to the plant dying as it is sensitive to the cold.
Harvest
As required. For choice, take non-flowering sprigs about 15cm in length.
Afterword
It is fun to topiary.

Opposite: Breadseed poppy mid-June.

Sage

We use this either as part of a chopped mixture of herbs to add to stews and sauces or on its own to add a special flavour to dishes. It's a favourite added to roast vegetables and goes particularly well with roast squash. If you don't want it to crisp away to charcoal add it late to the tray. It is delicious lightly fried in oil.

Rotation
Permanent.
Soil
Well-drained and moderately fertile.
Situation
Sunny.
Varieties
I grow two types. The purple sage is an attractive plant with beautiful flowers but the green broad-leaved sage has a superior flavour.
Sow
I haven't attempted this from seed.
Plant
Take softwood cuttings in May. Place 4 or 5 around the edge of a 9cm pot of free-draining compost. Pot them on into small pots, harden them off and set in their final places according to your purpose.

Care
For a continuous supply of healthy shoots for the kitchen, time the cutting back of the entire bush carefully. I have three green broad-leaved plants of different ages. One I cut back early in summer and one in late, and the other I leave pretty much alone until it gets straggly, and then cut it back in the spring. Cutting back in the autumn may kill the plant.
Harvest
Take shoots back as far as the leaves remain green and unblemished.
Afterword
Replace woody plants every few years.

Sorrel

Sorrel can be added to salad in small quantities, makes a wonderful soup and green sauce, and is a great accompaniment to oily fish. The lemony bite of sorrel is not however, to everyone's taste. I like it but, if you are at all prone to arthritis, limit the quantity you consume.

Rotation
Permanent. Divide plants if you wish to make a new bed.
Soil
Rich. Mine thrives on the edge of a fresh manure heap.
Situation
Sunny.
Varieties
Broad-leaf and buckler-leaf types.
Sow
In May in modules in the greenhouse.

Plant
Plant them 30cm apart. Both types will make large clumps.
Care
They can be invasive. Cut the flowering stems out to promote leaf production and to stop them self-seeding.
Harvest
Single leaves at a time.
Afterword
The texture of broad-leaf sorrel is just like skin.

Opposite: Sage in April.

Sweet Cicely

Practically the only use I have for my sweet cicely plant is for the leaves (spring) and seeds (summer) with stewed rhubarb. The seeds add a pleasant aniseed taste and both leaves and seeds reduce the amount of sugar that is needed.

Rotation
Permanent. Confine it to a tub and stop it from self-seeding. The roots can be impossible to get out once it becomes invasive.

Soil
Moderately rich and well drained.

Situation
It can handle some shade.

Varieties
Just the one.

Sow
In October prepare your tub by filling it with free-draining compost. Spread some seeds on the surface and cover them with compost. Place a sheet of glass over the tub and leave it outside. Make sure the compost does not dry out. Thin the plants to one or two per tub.

Plant
If planting out young seedlings space them 60cm apart.

Care
Be very careful to collect all the seed.

Harvest
The leaves in spring when the rhubarb is ready, and the seeds when they have ripened and turned black in summer for storage.

Afterword
It's an attractive plant but I do wonder if the space could be better used. Either that, or I need to become more adventurous in the kitchen.

Tarragon

This is another aniseed-flavoured herb. Single leaves can be stripped and added to leafy salads. As an ingredient in 'fines herbes' or on its own it is delicious added to egg and chicken dishes.

Rotation
Permanent.

Soil
Well drained. Low fertility is fine.

Situation
I have one clump in a sheltered position on the north side of some raised earth and another on the south side of the same raised earth, and the difference between the two is about three weeks in spring.

Varieties
French. Russian is not worth growing for cooking with.

Sow
Not from seed.

Plant
Dig up part of the patch in late May and settle it in somewhere else. As the plants mature the flavour fades so it is a good idea to renew them once every three or four years.

Care
Mulch with straw in winter.

Harvest
Fresh shoots about 15-20cm long. New growth is encouraged the more the plant is harvested.

Afterword
Worthwhile growing as it does not keep well once harvested and is seldom found in the market.

Opposite: Sweet Cicely in April.

Thyme

Thyme is a comfort to me. Maybe this has something to do with its anti-bacterial and anti-fungal properties. I love to put whole sprigs into slowly caramelising onions and lift the stalks out leaving all the leaves behind. It makes me feel clever. Orange and lemon thymes add interest to different dishes and teas.

Rotation
Permanent.

Soil
Well-drained and not too fertile.

Situation
Sunny.

Varieties
There are lots of varieties with different flavours.

Sow
Common garden thyme will self-seed.

Plant
It is easiest to buy plants that are of different culinary interest and allow them to self-seed or propagate from soft wood cuttings taken in spring.

Care
Keep the bushes well trimmed for a continuous supply of fresh shoots. Re-shape the bushes after flowering but don't cut into the hard wood or the bush will die back.

Harvest
The young shoots in spring are particularly tasty.

Afterword
Once you have established thyme that self-seeds, it is simply a question of weeding out what you don't want.

Winter Savory

This can be used in a mix with other strong-flavoured herbs. We use it as an ingredient in the dried pea and bean dishes that have become part of our hungry gap menu. It adds flavour and the reconstituted legumes become more digestible.

Rotation
Permanent.

Soil
Well-drained and not too rich.

Situation
Sunny.

Varieties
Just the one. I tried growing and using Summer Savory but found the flavour of the winter variety more to my taste.

Sow
An established plant will self-seed. Alternatively, seed may be sown in trays under cover in May.

Plant
Prick out and pot on small seedlings. Self-seeded plants can be dug up and re-planted when small. Space plants 30cm apart.

Care
Re-shape the plant when harvesting. Don't cut it back in the autumn as it is sensitive to the cold, and if you experience prolonged frosts protect the plant by surrounding it with straw.

Harvest
Non-flowering shoots 10-15cm long. It dries well and can be stored in an airtight jar for convenience.

Afterword
One of the most treasured plants in my herb garden.

Opposite: Winter Savory in April.

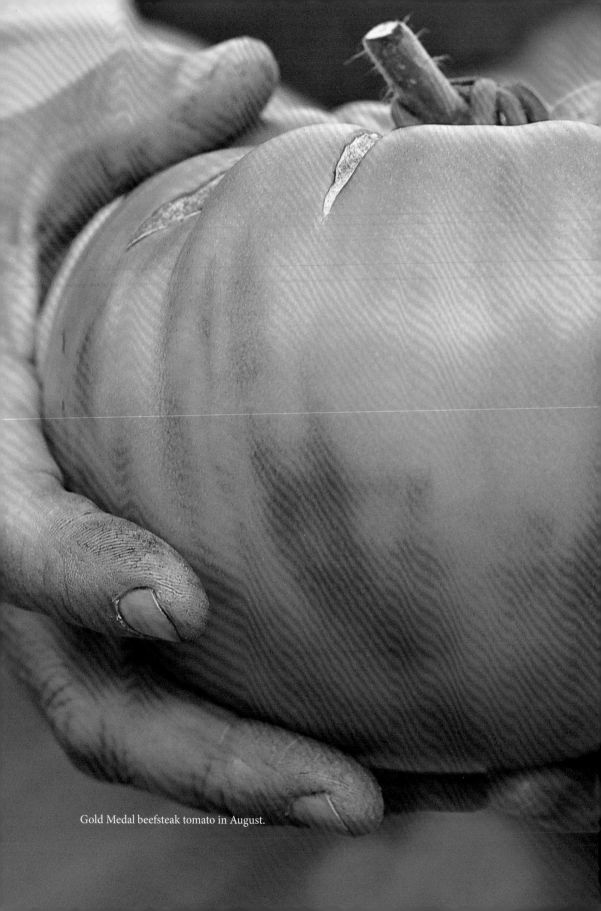
Gold Medal beefsteak tomato in August.

Chapter 4
alongside summer

Basil

Ocimum basilicum

I grow basil to harvest throughout the summer and to process into pesto. As early as March the seeds are scattered into a seed tray, covered lightly with compost and germinated on heat. When the seedlings are about 1cm tall they are pricked out 2.5cm each way into trays and grown on in an unheated greenhouse. When the young plants are growing on strongly they are planted out into the greenhouse border about 25cm from each other. The soil should be rich and well-drained, the plants watered regularly in the morning and the growing points picked every few days. Several kilos of leaf can be harvested from a dozen plants grown in this way throughout the summer and early autumn. At the end of the growing period (late October) the leaves are stripped off the plants and batch processed into pesto for the freezer.

Basil Pesto

Makes about nine person-sized portions but you may like more or less than we do.

1 clove garlic (or more if you like it)

3 tbsp pine nuts (or cashew nuts)

salt and pepper to taste

3 cups sweet basil (leaves only, well packed)

½ cup olive oil

½ cup grated parmesan

Combine the garlic, nuts, salt and pepper into a paste. Blend in the leaves of basil. Add the oil and lastly, the parmesan. Either store in sterilised jars with oil poured over the top of the paste in the fridge or, as I do, make portion-sized parcels for the freezer. Spoon a dollop on to a square of cling film. Fold the film over as if you were wrapping up sandwiches and twist each end. Settle four or more portions next to each other with the twisted ends pulled out to the sides in a plastic take-away tray and freeze them solid. They can be loosened after freezing and stored as 'free-flow' parcels in a bigger plastic bag.

Opposite: Sweet Basil in mid-July.

Runner beans

Phaseolus coccineus

I start my seeds off in root trainers at the end of April or early in May and plant them out at the base of a teepee after all danger of frost. They go in the legume rotation, and require a moderately rich moisture retentive soil and full sun. They are a favourite summer vegetable with many of the allotment holders on my site. We enjoy them fresh, usually sliced finely, steamed and with something with gravy (it takes all sorts!). I grow them particularly to make enough jars of chutney to see us through a winter of curries. This recipe is gluten free.

Bean chutney

1 kg fresh chopped runner beans

4 large chopped onions

1 kg Demerara sugar

1.5 tbsp corn-flour

1.5 tbsp English mustard

1.5 tbsp ground turmeric

750 ml malt vinegar

Cook the beans and onions in salted water until just tender and drain. Bring the beans and onions, sugar and 600 ml of the vinegar to the boil and simmer for 15 minutes. Mix the corn-flour, mustard and turmeric into the remaining vinegar and add to the main mix. Boil the complete mixture for a further 15 minutes. Pot the chutney into sterilised jars and seal them as if you were making jam. A handy tip is to serve the chutney in a dish. If you leave the whole jar out when your Dad comes round you have to be prepared to face the consequences.

Opposite: Runner bean Wisley Magic in August.

Broad beans

Vicia faba

Planted in October, both Super Aquadulce and Crimson-flowered broad beans over-winter well and produce their first pods to harvest in early June. Spring plantings will give a succession of beans and an excess will freeze. To my taste they are one of the very few vegetables that freeze well enough to be acceptable on their own steamed from frozen. Alternatively, leave the beans to mature and harvest the dried beans for use in the same way as Yin Yang or Bosnian varieties mentioned in the A-Z chapter. Broad beans have similar soil and situation requirements as French beans and occupy the legume rotation. They are nitrogen fixers so leave the roots in the soil when clearing the beds. They can be followed by hardy varieties of lettuce that are neutral in the rotation, or by kale or other brassicas such as spring cabbages if the beans are not cleared from the beds until later in the summer.

To free-flow freeze broad beans

Harvest the pods when the skins of the beans are still soft and palatable. Bring a pan full of water to the boil and add a small quantity of the freshly-podded beans so that the water is maintained close to the boil. Blanche the beans for one and a half minutes from the time they first enter the water. Drain the water away (into another pan that can go back on the heat if you have several batches to do) and immediately immerse the beans in ice-cold water. When the heat has gone out of the beans, drain them and place them on a clean tea towel to soak up excess water. Make a single layer of beans on a tray. Place the tray in the freezer and when the beans are solid transfer them to a plastic bag or container within the freezer. Peas also do quite well with this method.

Opposite: Broad bean Super Aquadulce flowers in the third week of May.

Chilli peppers

Capsicum annuum

I start chilli pepper seeds in February at the same time as tomatoes in rows in a seed tray of multipurpose compost on heat in our east-facing conservatory. They are slower to germinate than tomatoes and, to my mind, more difficult to grow well. Prick them out into 9cm pots when they are large enough to handle. Keep them warm and well-lit for another 4-8 weeks before transferring them to an unheated greenhouse. Water them, taking care that they don't get too wet and check them daily for greenfly. Pot the young plants on when their roots show at the bottom of the pot, increasing the size of the pot gradually to encourage new roots. Mine stay in a sheltered place in their pots throughout the summer and early autumn. I grow enough to use fresh and air dry. Dried chillies are broken up and stored in a jar in the spice drawer or placed under sunflower oil to make hot oil for general use when cooking. One of our must-haves for the store cupboard is my friend Judy's chilli sauce.

Chilli sauce

24 large ripe tomatoes

4 onions

2 green peppers

3 red peppers

1 bunch celery (or leaf celery)

4 cups white sugar

2 cups distilled vinegar

3 tbsp salt

3 tsp of pickling spice in a bag (dried chilli, cardamom etc.)

2-4 little red chilli peppers, to taste

Place all in one pot over a low heat. Stir. It takes about 3 hours to mush down and looks fairly solid and red. Spoon into sterilised jars while still hot and seal the jars as if for jam. Judy says this is good with egg-fried rice, hamburgers, anything. We like it with re-fried beans and it is excellent with barbequed food in the summer.

Opposite: Chilli pepper at the beginning of November.

Gherkins

Cucumis sativus

Gherkins are started early in May at the same time as other cucumbers, courgettes and squashes. Sow single seeds (or two per pot if using old seed: thin to one per pot) in 9cm pots of multipurpose compost on heat. Soon after germination transfer them to an unheated greenhouse and pot them on when their roots show at the bottom of the pot. They are neutral in the rotation and enjoy a rich, well-drained soil in full sun. Pick the fruits when they are about the size of a 50 pence piece in diameter for the recipe below. Pick them smaller than this if you are pickling them whole.

Winnipeg bread and butter pickles

4 quarts (4400ml) of sliced cucumbers

1 quart (1100ml) sliced onions

brine to cover the veg made by dissolving 1 cup salt in 9 cups of water

weak solution of equal parts vinegar and water

Pickling syrup

4.5 cups of brown sugar

1.5 cups of water

3.5 cups of vinegar

1 tsp celery seed

1 tsp mustard seed

1 tsp turmeric

Soak the vegetables in separate bowls in brine overnight. Next morning drain the brine away and cook the veg, just covered, in the weak solution of vinegar. Heat the mixture for 10 minutes and do not allow the temperature to rise above simmering. Drain the solution away and pack the veg into sterilised jars. To make the pickling syrup dissolve the brown sugar in the water and vinegar, add the celery seed, mustard seed and turmeric, and bring all to boiling point. Pour over the packed veg and seal while the jars are still warm. Fantastic in sandwiches.

Opposite: Gherkins in August.

Raspberries - autumn

Rubus idaeus

The autumn raspberry Joan J has large fruits, tastes terrific and will crop until November or later. Other autumn varieties are good too. Raspberries are permanent in the rotation. I mulch with well-rotted manure in the spring after cutting them to the ground in February. They will stand a bit of shade.

If you want to start a bed and be sure of virus-free stock then order in some canes and plant them whenever they arrive. If you are extending your patch do this in February before cutting them down. Drive your spade firmly into the soil between a main plant and a runner until the root that links them together has been sliced through. Lift the new cane with its root and place it in a hole you prepared earlier. Add a good spade full of well rotted manure to the planting hole and a shake of bonemeal to stimulate root growth. Mix it and settle in your new cane to the level at which it was already growing. Water it well if the soil is dry and firm the soil in around the roots. Plant new canes at least 60cm apart. Some people cut the cane off at about a foot in the first year but one year I forgot to do this and cut them all to the ground as I do for established plants and they still fruited well in their first year.

If you grow autumn raspberries you don't need to put them in a fruit cage. The blackbirds take the odd one here at the start of the season but after this they leave them alone. Be ruthless with removing runners. If your patch fills up with plants your berries will be smaller. They are generally trouble-free but I did have a problem one year with a tortrix moth that stripped the leaves off the plants. I started again with fresh canes some distance away.

They free-flow freeze easily if set out on trays, and can be enjoyed for breakfast and pudding throughout the year. They also make wonderful jam and wine.

Raspberry jam

1 to 2 Kg of fruit - depends on the size of your pot

the same quantity of sugar as fruit

You can reduce the proportion of sugar to fruit but then the jam has to be kept in the fridge. Place the raspberries in a pot over a medium low heat and warm them slowly at first. Increase the heat as the fruit breaks down. Warm the sugar slightly in the oven. Keep an eye on it – I overdid this one year and ended up with a roasting tray half full of caramel. Add the sugar to the fruit and stir until all the sugar is dissolved. Stop stirring and turn up the heat. Bring the mixture to a rolling boil. Remove froth that surfaces with a flat spoon. With small amounts of fruit the setting point is arrived at very quickly so start testing it after 2 minutes and have your jars hot and your sterilised lids ready. I let the jam cool very slightly before pouring it into the jars. Put the lids on immediately.

Opposite: Raspberry jam on toast.

Tomatillos

Physalis ixocarpa

These grow well here under cover or in a sheltered spot outside. I start them off at the same time as my tomato seeds in a seed tray lightly covered with multipurpose compost on heat. They get potted on and planted out into the border soil of the polytunnel. They appear more fragile than tomatoes but soon thicken up to form bushy plants up to 90cm tall and of a similar diameter, so leave this distance between your plants. I surround 4-5 plants with stakes and rope to stop them from lolling about. They are members of the Solanaceae and so occupy the potato rotation. They don't suffer from any obvious problems and the fruits should be harvested just before they fall off the plant. These fruits, so similar to tomatoes, but unlike them in flavour, are a bit of an acquired taste and we have acquired it. There are many salsa recipes with tomatillos as they are popular in Mexico. Here is one of our favourites.

Tomatillo salsa

50g onions

250g tomatillos

50g sweet pepper

1-3 medium hot chillies

1 tsp coriander leaf

2 tbsp cider or cider vinegar

salt

2 tbsp vegetable oil

1 tsp sugar

Chop all the vegetable ingredients very finely. Pieces between 3 and 5mm cubed are ideal. Chop the coriander very finely. Combine with the cider, salt, oil and sugar. The juices flow and mingle and the result is wonderfully fresh, sharp and savoury all at once. Store in a jar in the fridge or freeze in portions in the freezer.

Opposite: Tomatillos growing in the polytunnel in late July.

Tomatoes

Lycopersicon esculentum

Dried in the sun or a low oven or reduced to sauce and then bottled or frozen, tomatoes get added to casseroles, pasta, curries and pizza throughout the year. Often accompanied by basil pesto, our diet would be impoverished without this wonderful summer vegetable that is really a fruit. Tomatoes are my weakness. There are so many heritage and other varieties to try, each with its own personality. I grow a dozen or more different varieties every year and every year I try different ones. They are started off in multipurpose compost in February on heat and potted on to their final growing place under cover in May. They like a rich moisture-retentive well-drained soil and plenty of sun. Sink the last pot the plant was in next to it and water into this so that you can monitor what you do. Feed with comfrey liquid twice weekly. Harvest them when fully ripe for the best flavour. The recipe that follows is generic. Whatever happens to be available goes in there. Of course it is no accident that whatever is available is seasonally compatible, so the product will already be familiar to many of you.

Pasta sauce

500g or more fully ripe tomatoes, skins removed and chopped roughly

1-2 medium-sized onions (or shallots)

1-3 cloves of garlic squashed under a teaspoon of salt

a slurp of oil (olive or sunflower)

sprigs of thyme (or other herbs that you like)

up to 100g of other veg such as French beans or peas or courgettes

Sweat the onions and garlic in the oil and when they are soft add the tomatoes and herbs. Simmer over a low heat until the tomatoes have reduced. Add the other vegetables and cook them through. If you use soft herbs such as basil or parsley add them after reducing the sauce and cook briefly for a further two minutes. Set aside to cool and freeze in a solid plastic container. Transfer the block of sauce after it has frozen to a freezer bag and label. If you use the same size containers each time they will stack very economically in the freezer. Alternatively the sauce may be bottled and sealed in sterilised jars.

Opposite: Tomatoes in August.

veg sowing and planting calendar

	january	february	march	april	may
artichoke-globe			s/p	p	p
artichoke-jerusalem		p	p	p	p
asparagus		p	s/p	s	
bean (broad/process)					
bean (French/drying)					s
bean (runner/process)				s	s
beetroot				s	s
broccoli				s	s
brussels sprout				s	
cabbage (spring)					
cabbage (winter)					s
carrot		s(cover)			
cauliflower					s
celeriac		s(heat)			
chard & perpetual spinach					
chicory & endive					
chilli pepper (process)		s(heat)	s(heat)		
garlic					
gherkin (process)					s
kale				s	s
leek			s	s	
lettuce					
onion (main)		s(heat)	s/p(sets)	s/p(sets)	
onion ('spring')					
onion (Welsh)				p	
parsnip				s	
pea (drying)		s	s		
pea (shoots)					
potato (main)				p	
radish (2 types)		s(salad)			
raspberry (process)		p	p		
rhubarb	p	p	p	p	
salad leaves					
seakale			p(cuttings)	s(seeds)	
shallot		p(cover)	p(sets)	p(sets)	
spinach (soft)					
squash				s(heat)	s
tomato (process)		s(heat)	s(heat)		
tomatillo (process)		s(heat)	s(heat)		
turnip					

june	july	august	september	october	november	december
				s	s	
s						
s	s					
	s					
	s(main)		s(cover)			
s	s	s				
s	s	s	s(cover)	s(cover)		
				p		
		s	s	p(cover)	p(cover)	
	s(seeds)		p(o/w sets)			
			s(cover)	s(cover)		
			s(cover)	s(cover)	s(cover)	s(cover)
	s	s(cover)	s(cover)			
				p	p	p
	s	s	s			
					take cuttings	
		s	s			
			s(cover)	s(cover)		

additional sowing and planting notes

You may wish to add your summer plan here.

	january	february	march	april	may

june	july	august	september	october	november	december

Resources

There are excellent books out there and a quick search on the internet will satisfy many of you. The books below are ones I have collected over the years and refer to frequently. Within each category titles are arranged according to date of publication. Almost all of them are still available.

General vegetable growing

Vegetable and herb growing
The Culture of Vegetables and Flowers from Seeds and Roots
Sutton and Sons of Reading, 1930 Eighteenth Edition, Simpkin Marshall Ltd
   A thoroughly practical A to Z of vegetables (herbs under H) and a month by month guide to tasks. Early techniques still relevant today are explained and useful details for the hungry gap gardener will be found. The culture of flowers is laid out. Handsome line drawings of common pests and diseases Illustrate a late section of the book. The remedies veer from totally unacceptable to those used in contemporary organic practice.

Plain Vegetable Growing
George E. Whitehead, 1941, Adam and Charles Black
   This is a vegetable book so simple a child could understand it.

Asparagus: Bulletin No. 60 of the Ministry of Agriculture and Fisheries
Ed. by Mr F. A. Secrett, Chairman of the Vegetable Group of the National Agricultural Advisory Service, 1949, His Majesty's Stationery Office
   An account of asparagus growing in Britain at this time illustrated by line drawings and photographs.

The Vegetable Garden Displayed
Compiled and Published by the Royal Horticultural Society, 1961
   There is much here of use to the hungry gap gardener. This book is stunningly illustrated by 'nearly three hundred photographs'. The carrot clamp, beetroot tub, onion ropes and haricot bean bundles are objects of great beauty.

The Complete Vegetable Grower
W. E. Shewell-Cooper, 1973, Faber and Faber Ltd
   First published in 1955, this book has a section on green manure and crop rotation that is more than ever relevant to gardening practice today.

The Gardener's Book of Weeds
Mea Allan, 1978, MacDonald and Jane's Publishers Limited
   An excellent reference on weeds. The use of common names as well as botanical ones make this book easy to use.

Oriental Vegetables: the Complete Guide for Garden and Kitchen
Joy Larkcom, 1991, John Murray (Publishers) Ltd
   The growing information chart near the end of the book makes it easy to see at a glance which varieties are possible for hungry gap use.

The Allotment Gardener's Handbook
Alan Titchmarsh, 1991, Treasure Press
  Straightforward practical advice presented clearly.

Your Garden Week by Week
Arthur Hellyer, 1992, Chancellor Press
  Reprinted several times since 1936. Information on flowers and vegetables. Ideas about the use of peat and insecticides have now changed, but should you want to check the time for setting onion seed for exhibition, this is your book. It is a little difficult to use it to grow for the hungry gap as you would need several place-markers to gather the information you need on any one vegetable.

Vegetables
Roger Phillips and Martyn Rix, 1993, Macmillan
  How vegetables developed from their wild origins. There is a section on plant families useful for gardeners struggling to sort out their rotation.

Creative Vegetable Gardening
Joy Larkcom, 1997, Mitchell Beazley
  This is a beautiful book. Its hungry gap relevance is in the outstanding photographs in the A-Z directory towards the back. More realistic than drawings, these images were the first to really bring alive for me the lesser known kales and salad greens it is possible to grow outside and under unheated cover.

The Royal Horticultural Society: Pests and Diseases
Pippa Greenwood and Andrew Halstead, 1997, Dorling Kindersley Limited
  This is my first port of call in trouble. There is an emphasis on prevention.

Bob Flowerdew's Complete Book of Companion Gardening
Bob Flowerdew, 1998 (revised edition), Kyle Cathie Limited
  This is a good read if you want to find out about companion planting.

Heritage vegetables: the gardener's guide to cultivating diversity
Sue Stickland, 1998, Gaia Books Limited
  Sue Stickland is definitely one of my gardening heroes and this book is a glimpse into the treasure chest of vegetables from past and present.

The Vegetable & Herb Expert
Dr D. G. Hessayon, 2000, Expert Books
  Very good general advice and possible to pick up second hand.

Back Garden Seed Saving: Keeping Our Vegetable Heritage Alive
Sue Stickland, 2001, eco-logic books
  If you are looking for details about how to keep your saved seed true then you will find them here. Thirty-three crops are covered and many interesting varieties mentioned together with the guardians dedicated to keeping our vegetable heritage alive.

The Heligan Vegetable Bible
Tim Smit & Phillip McMillan Browse, 2002, Cassell Illustrated

The inspirational story of the reconstruction of the walled garden at Heligan. It includes the process of sourcing vegetable varieties appropriate to the Victorian era to cultivate. Beautiful photographs.

The Royal Horticultural Society: Fruit and Vegetable Gardening
Ed. by Michael Pollock, 2002, Dorling Kindersley Limited

If I were allowed only one gardening book I would choose this one.

Growing Unusual Vegetables
Simon Hickmott, 2003, eco-logic books

Valuable advice on how to cultivate lesser known crops.

Valuable Vegetables: Gardening for pleasure and for profit...
Mandy Pullen, 2004, eco-logic books

Useful advice even if you have no intention of selling your produce. There are easy tips to follow for maintaining fertility, growing green manures and figuring out a rotation that suits you. The emphasis is on sustainability.

Jekka's Complete Herb Book
Jekka McVicar, revised edition 2007, Kyle Cathie Limited

This book is fantastically knowledgeable, instantly accessible and beautifully illustrated with some stunning photographs. I refer to it frequently.

The Biodynamic sowing and planting calendar XXXX
Maria & Matthias Thun, Floris Books

A necessary part of my toolkit. This needs to be bought annually.

Gardening under cover

Plastic and Vegetables: A guide to Organic Growing in Polytunnels
David Storey, 1993, Irish Organic Farmers and Growers Association (IOFGA)

I used this small book to get started in polytunnel growing. There are home recipes for equisetum tea, and nettle remedies for botrytis and aphids.

Gardening Under Plastic: How to use Fleece, Films, Cloches and Polytunnels
Bernard Salt, 2001, Batsford (Anova) Books

If you are just starting with a polytunnel this book is rich with detail about how to put one up, what to grow and pests, diseases and disorders to look out for. Useful sections on cloches, setting seed in pots, pricking out and potting on.

'Grow and Cook' books & Cook books

Domestic Preservation of Fruit and Vegetables: Bulletin Number 21 of the Ministry of Agriculture and Fisheries
Miss M. L. Adams and colleagues, 1938 (first issued in 1929), His Majesty's Stationery Office

Advice on bottling and canning fruit and vegetables is to be found here. Jam-making and jelly recipes as well as instructions on how to make fruit syrups, crystallised fruits and dried fruits are included. Chutney and pickle recipes ensure that absolutely all of the summer excess is preserved for the winter. (I was lucky enough to see a friend's copy.)

Food From Your Garden: All you need to know to grow, cook and preserve your own fruit and vegetables
Edited, designed and published by the Reader's Digest Association Limited, 1977

This book does exactly what it says on the cover. It includes a step-by-step illustrated guide for wine-making that is excellent for beginners. Our own copy was picked up second-hand and since then we have found a further two copies to give to friends.

Grow and Cook
Violet Stevenson, 1979, Coronet Books/Hodder and Stoughton

Organised as an A-Z, this small paperback contains details of timing as well as practical suggestions for growing, and ideas for how to use gluts. For example, in the section on carrots, glazed carrots, carrot jam and carrot wine feature. However no mention is made of carrot fly in her outline of how to grow carrots - maybe it wasn't such a problem then.

Jane Grigson's Vegetable Book
Jane Grigson, 1980, Penguin Books

Jane Grigson's encyclopaedic knowledge of vegetables is awesome. You will find historical culinary detail, how to choose and prepare your roots, shoots and leaves for classical and contemporary dishes. She inserts gardening advice into her text by way of references to other sources.

Preserving
Oded Schwartz, 1996, Dorling Kindersley Limited

We have tried several of the recipes from this book with great success. Almost every year I make Shallot Confiture.

The Food We Eat
Joanna Blythman, 1996, Michael Joseph Ltd

If you need reminding about why you garden organically then dip into this investigative account about how most of the food in supermarkets is treated.

The Herbfarm Cookbook
Jerry Traunfeld, 2000, Scribner

Great recipes, a chart indicating the season of use for salad ingredients including herbs, flowers and leaves, and another showing the growing requirements of 31 herbs are included here. One of my favourite cook books.

Sophie Grigson's Herbs
Sophie Grigson, 2000, BBC Worldwide Ltd

Useful ideas for recipes with herbs. There is a section on edible flowers some of which are available towards the end of the hungry gap.

Salad Leaves for all Seasons

Charles Dowding, 2008, Green Books Ltd

If you decide to specialise in salad leaves then this is essential reading. It features timetables for all year round indoor and outdoor sowing, sustaining and harvesting. Single leaf harvesting is the most valuable tip I have taken from this book.

Winemaking

First Steps in Winemaking

C. J. J. Berry, 1980, Amateur Winemaker Publications Ltd

This is an excellent month-by-month guide to winemaking. I have tried several of the recipes from this book and have had one failure in the past 12 years.

Making Wild Wines and Meads

Pattie Vargas & Rich Gulling, 1999, Storey Books

The elderflower recipes in this book are something special.

Self-sufficiency

On Next to Nothing: A Guide to Survival Today

Thomas and Susan Hinde, 1976, Book Club Associates

Much more is commented on than vegetables and fruit and if you are considering livestock there are some useful tips. Our copy falls open at the page with the recipe for Pommes de Terre a L'Ardennaise, a delicious way to eat potatoes in the winter.

Cost-Effective Self-Sufficiency or The Middle-Class Peasant

Eve and Terence McLaughlin, 1978, David and Charles

Should you wish to go as far as building your own solar panel or windmill then this is a starting point. Instructions for building your own cold frame, propagator base or hot bed are included.

The Concise Book of Organic Growing and Small Livestock

Meike and David Watkins, 1983

Serious about attempting 'the good life'? Get yourself 3 to 4 acres of land and a copy of this book. It comes with a do-it- yourself moon planting guide.

The Complete Book of Self-Sufficiency

John Seymour, 1996, Dorling Kindersley Limited

This is the book I would keep from this section.

Photography

The Internet brings us seemingly unlimited images at the click of a mouse and if you are interested in photography you will have your own favourite sources. Here are two books that have been influential during the course of this project.

Plant Kingdoms: the photographs of Charles Jones

Sean Sexton – Robert Flynn Johnson, 1998, Smithmark Publishers

I identify with this gardener who harvested his cabbages and root vegetables and posed them in front of his camera to take their portraits. I have never yet seen, nor have I been able to make a photograph of carrots as beautiful as the one at the beginning of this book. I too would have used my glass plates for cloches if that was what was to hand.

Darkroom to Digital: Black and white photography with photoshop – the art of transition

Eddie Ephraums, 2005, Argentum

This book gave me confidence while making the leap into digital photography from a film-based practice.

Seed suppliers

Below is a list of some seed companies I have experience of; favourites first.

www.OrganicCatalogue.com

Very reliable. Members get 10% discount. See also The Heritage Seed Library (HSL) accessible through the Garden Organic website. www.gardenorganic.org.uk

www.realseeds.co.uk

This company offers advice on summer sowing and seed saving. They really want you to feed yourself the whole year round with open pollinated varieties.

www.seedsofitaly.com

Good for endives and chicories. Their organic range is listed separately, varieties suitable for winter cultivation are highlighted in blue and their seed packets are very generous.

www.Marshalls-seeds.co.uk

Very well laid out website. Good on cabbages.

www.Thompson-Morgan.com

Includes a great range of seeds for sprouting. All veg is not necessarily organic.

www.suttons.co.uk

I think this website is organised beautifully and easier to use than the printed version.

www.mr-fothergills.co.uk

Some unusual varieties stocked.

Suffolk Herbs, Tel.01376 572456 & King's Seeds, Tel. 01376 570000

I find the printed version of their catalogue easier to use than their website.

Chervil in the snow.

Notes

notes

notes

notes

Index

Acknowledgements

I would like to thank all those who had a hand in teaching me about growing vegetables: my Mum, my partner Jan Pearse, and all gardeners who have found the time to communicate and write about what they know. Friends who have eaten and appreciated the vegetables I grow are important. In particular, a special thanks to Jill for writing the foreword; I am very moved by her words.

Thanks also to my photographic course-mates at the local library and our wonderful teacher Julia Rafferty for help and comments over the course of this project. My friend Judy Wolfram for her recipes, enthusiasm and help in getting the book 'out there' has been terrific. Thanks to Reen Pilkington, Ursula Howard and Stephen Yeo for invaluable feedback on the text, design and the practicality of my offerings. I am lucky to have friends with such a wealth of expertise.

Thanks to Mike, Joe and Danny at Crowes Printers for their generous advice, and their gentle treatment of an anxious novice.

Above: Bishy Barnabee.